Betrayal of Trust

The Father Brendan Smyth Affair
and the Catholic Church

Chris Moore

Foreword by Kevin Hegarty

First published in 1995 by
Marino Books
An imprint of Mercier Press
16 Hume Street Dublin 2

Trade enquiries to Mercier Press
PO Box 5, 5 French Church Street,
Cork

A Marino Original

© Chris Moore 1995
© Foreword Kevin Hegarty

ISBN 1 86023 027 X

10 9 8 7 6 5 4 3 2 1

A CIP record for this title is available
from the British Library

Cover design by Bluett
Set by Richard Parfrey
Printed in Ireland by ColourBooks,
Baldoyle Industrial Estate, Dublin 13

CONTENTS

	Acknowledgements	4
	Foreword by Kevin Hegarty	5
	Introduction	15
1	Kilnacrott	21
2	In the Beginning . . .	31
3	Betrayal of Trust	40
4	Back to School	53
5	Porn in the USA	66
6	Langdon City Limits	79
7	Pursuit of the Truth	98
8	Turn Away. Don't Look at Me.	120
9	The Burden of Guilt	135
10	Chasing Shadows 1: Priest on the Run	143
11	Chasing Shadows 2: Church on the Run	171
12	Fr Bruno: the Whistle-Blower	199
13	A Government Falls	228

ACKNOWLEDGEMENTS

That this work was produced at all is due for the most part to the encouragement I received at home from my wife Fiona. In spite of my realisation that I was a reporter and not a writer she kept me going in those darkest moments. But thanks are due to others for their support: to all my colleagues at UTV's *Counterpoint* office (Michael Beattie, Tony Curry, Michael Nesbitt, Paul Robinson, Ken Devlin, Mary Curry); especially to our production secretary/assistant Mary McCleave for all her kind words in the face of lengthy transcripts of recorded material; to the management of UTV for encouraging this work; to my mother-in-law Mary Boyd who reminded a weary old news hack of the need to recognise years of journalistic neglect and understanding of proper sentence punctuation; to my father Billy for taking time to read and correct the early manuscripts; to Fr Kevin Hegarty for his understanding encouragement; and to the staff at Marino (Jo, Anne, Siobhan, Bernie and Sean) for their tolerance and assistance in making this book a reality.

Special appreciation is due to the abused and their families for all the time and assistance they offered to make the telling of their story possible. *Betrayal of Trust* is for those Fr Brendan Smyth abused, a tribute to their courage in finding voice for their grievances and in seeking justice against all the odds.

This book is dedicated with love to my children, Jason, Steven and Louise, for their encouragement over many years of long hours and missing days.

FOREWORD

My favourite fairytale is 'The Emperor with No Clothes'. You will recall it tells of a vain and foolish emperor duped by crooked tailors into parting with an enormous sum of money for a non-existent but supposedly exquisite gown. When he wore the 'gown' on parade in the capital city the cheering crowds colluded in the deception – except for a young boy who had the temerity to blurt out that the emperor was naked.

All powerful institutions and individuals require for their purification someone to say uncomfortable things and ask awkward questions. In this gripping account of Fr Brendan Smyth's trail of child abuse for over thirty years Chris Moore fulfils this function for a venerable Irish institution, the Catholic Church. Brendan Smyth is now serving a sentence for his activities but the wider question of Church accountability lingers stubbornly in the air.

The Catholic Church was once the dominant force in our public life, its self-confidence structurally symbolised by the imposing Victorian Gothic cathedrals that over-shadow many Irish towns. It is now in some decline because of the crumbling of the alliance of conservative nationalism, middle-class economics and religion that gave birth to the Irish state. The Church has so far failed to develop a coherent and consistent pastoral response to the impulses that animate Irish society today. Several factors have converged to cause crisis in Irish Catholicism but, in my opinion, none has been as significant as the recent spate of child sexual abuse allegations, of which so far the Brendan Smyth affair has been the most extensive and best documented. They strike at the heart of the priest-people relationship. It is correct but of little avail to say that statistically a celibate is less likely to molest a child than a married person, for in Catholic culture a higher standard is always expected of the priest, both as person and professional. Furthermore, people are shocked that the Church establishment, often a stern dispenser of moral wisdom, has been culpable and inept in its response to the abuse allegations. And as it seems to many that the truth was only reluctantly dragged into the public arena, there remains the suspicion, perhaps unwarranted but nonetheless real, that there are further dark secrets to be revealed.

To appreciate the dismay of Irish Catholics about the child abuse revelations it is necessary to understand the priest-people relationship in the Catholic community. I refer in the main to rural Ireland, the world with which I am most familiar. In 'Station Island' Seamus Heaney captures the everyday reality of the relationship:

Visiting neighbours.
Drinking tea and praising home made bread
Something in them would be ratified
When they saw you at the door in your black suit
arriving like some sort of holy mascot.

In the traditional Irish family a priest member was a sign of status, a symbol of upward social mobility. People often share their most vulnerable moments with priests. In the confessional they may be privy to the deepest secrets of the community - one thinks of Graham Greene's evocative comment about the Curé of Ars committing to his mind the impurity of a province. They are honoured participants in people's most meaningful rites - invited to perform baptisms, brought to the top table at weddings, deemed necessary at death to give ecclesiastical discipline to shapeless sorrow. In the Irish Republic priests in parishes are almost invariably chairpersons of boards of management of national schools. They have immediate access to schools and are usually trusted by parents, teachers and children.

This relationship, clearly rooted, has not been destroyed by what has been revealed recently. As Bishop Willie Walsh wrote in *The Furrow* (February 1995): 'People quickly distinguish between image and reality. The reality for them is the priest they see on Sunday, the priest who visited mother when in hospital, the priest who cried with us when we lost our child, the priest who didn't pass our door even though he knew we were not married in church.' It would be foolish to pretend, however, that the corporate image of priesthood has not been severely dented. Sociological surveys in America indicate a loss of trust in the priest-people relationship as a result of child abuse revelations. To my knowledge no such surveys have been published here but I sense from listening to people that the effect here has been similar. In November 1994 *The Sunday Tribune* reported that when a priest in a Dublin diocese knocked at a door during parish visitation the young man who answered said 'Sorry, Father, there are no children in this house,' and slammed the door. That is obviously an exaggerated reaction but it has found less dramatic echoes throughout the country. The sense of betrayal was most forcefully articulated in the spring number of *Studies*, in which Seán Ó Conaill reflects the pain of committed Catholics that 'the clerical Church . . . has harboured the greatest evil its children could suffer within its own ranks and made it impossible for them to break free by its own clerically dominated culture. . . that it was less effective than secular agencies in delivering justice to its most innocent and vulnerable members. . . and in light of the clergy's long-expressed idealisation of the family as the most vital social unit, the revelation that these families were not protected by the Church, were instead its victims, has been staggering.'

How can the Church assuage the pain that has been caused, restore the trust that has been broken? How can we use our resources and talents, our gifts and our faith, to address issues of deep hurt and become channels of healing where we have, through dysfunction, been facilit-ators of harm? Our primary concern must be for the victims. As some lines by Derek Mahon ('A Disused Shed in County Wexford') express in another context:

They are begging us you see
in their wordless way
To do something, to speak on their behalf,
Or at least not to close the door again.

Nothing can alleviate the pain they have suffered or restore the innocence they have lost but the Church must support every effort for their rehabilitation. Nor must the Catholic Church disown the perpetrators of abuse from within its ranks. In the anger at the damage they have caused it can be forgotten that they too are victims – victims often of psychological problems and impoverished seminary formation programmes that failed to identify their proclivities. Any form of ostracism is out of kilter with the Christian imperative to hate the sin but love the sinner.

It is fair to recognise that the Irish Church is making some effort to redress the scandal of child abuse. There have been episcopal statements and pastoral letters read in churches. A committee of experts has been established to draw up guidelines and in the case of Brendan Smyth's Abbot there has been a resignation. Cardinal Daly has stated: 'We are in mourning for the sins of our brethren, who have betrayed us all but above all betrayed their innocent victims. We are in mourning for the innocent children and families on whom hurt and harm have been so wantonly inflicted.' Yet I think that the response of the Irish Church lacks symbolic power compared, for example, to the action of Bishop Harry Flynn from the diocese of Lafayette in Louisiana. This diocese became the focus of intense media interest in 1984, when Fr Gilbert Gauthe became the first priest in the United States to be exposed as a child molester. Details of Fr Gauthe's behaviour was revealed, other priest perpetrators were identified and the Church was accused of a cover-up. Before Flynn's arrival as bishop the parishioners of Lafayette were understandably devastated. He made it a priority to address the trauma caused by the scandal. He met and continues to meet each victim. He visited affected parishes. He offered Mass and spoke to parishioners directly about the revelations. He encouraged victims of clerical misconduct to come forward and offers an annual Mass in the cathedral for all victims of violence and abuse.

The Brendan Smyth case and allied scandals raise fundamental questions that are germane to the revelations but also wider-ranging: on the culture of secrecy in the Church, on seminary formation, on the need to develop a theology and practice which stresses the rights and dignity of children. Should the Church address these questions I am convinced that the present crisis would be a period of purification for it.

I believe that one reason why these scandals took so long to reach the public arena is connected to the culture of secrecy in the Church. There is a widespread impression that the Church establishment is an exclusive and secretive male club, the members of which are embedded in each other's prejudices and indulge each other's foibles. This impression contains enough of the truth to be worrying. In such a culture, criticism is seen as not only inconvenient but disloyal. When I was editor of the Catholic Church magazine *Intercom*, I published a temperate article on clerical child abuse, six months before the Brendan Smyth affair surfaced, which incurred severe episcopal disapproval. Allied to this undue emphasis on secrecy, the Church also suffers from the tyranny of deference among the laity. It has been said that when a man becomes a bishop he never again lacks for a good meal and never again hears the truth. This may be pleasant but it is radically unhealthy. What is needed is a Church which is open and encourages lay people to have a real input into decision-making.

Among priests there is general dissatisfaction with seminary training. The aim of traditional formation was to produce strong military-type men who could easily eschew intimate human contact. Priests were schooled in what has recently been dubbed as the 'John Wayne school of rugged individualism'. I am reminded of the priest in the Jack B. Yeats sketch looming in solitary splendour over his little community. In a recent *cri de coeur* in *The Sunday Press*, Colm Kilcoyne struck a chord that resonates with may priests and seminarians today:

> In seven years in Maynooth I never had a minute's advice on how to live celibacy and still stay normal and warm. In thirty-five years as a priest, I have never been at a local conference in our diocese where we talked openly and honestly about celibacy. We have discussed FÁS schemes, school management, divorce, pensions, drugs and emigration until you'd be fit to scream. But never, ever, a session on how to live something that profoundly influences your way of life. So I have huge sympathy for priests who stray and for the women who get involved and then get hurt. We are dealing here with men who have little or no training in sexual delicacy. Is it any wonder that their relationships often get messy, manipulative and end in tears.

Seminary formation must become more responsive to the human needs of those aspiring to be priests. There is a need in our seminaries for comprehensive vocational preparation programmes which use modern psychological insights into the human personality and are respectful of Christian traditions. These programmes would enable students to overcome the blocks that are an obstacle to them becoming free and loving persons and would identify these with severe sexual problems. A calling like the priesthood, which by its nature is often concerned with people in confidential and vulnerable situations, demands no less. Priests can function as 'wounded healers' only when they have become aware of and sought healing for their own wounds.

Finally, I believe that the Irish Church needs to develop a theology and practice which stresses the dignity of children. The Church emphasises the dignity of the individual from conception to death. In recent years in Ireland it seems to me that more energy has been expended on the right to life of the child in the womb than on the quality of life for children after they are born. Children need space where they can speak their truth. Where children feel they will not be listened to or disparaged they are vulnerable and become disempowered. Some words of Anne Thurston in her recent book *Because of Her Testimony* (Gill and Macmillan) could serve as an inspiration for a new way of seeing children:

If the understanding of the Christian community is that the Kingdom is a place of hospitality for the weak and the vulnerable and the marginalised then children have a right to lay claim to it. In our treatment of the physically 'little' among us we communicate our understanding of the priorities and values in our society. When children are loved as separate others, not possessed as 'precious objects' or rejected as insignificant, they learn to inhabit a world where they are utterly confident that despite pain, in the end 'everything will be all right'.

Though he may not be thanked for it, Chris Moore has done the Irish Church some service in his exposé of the Brendan Smyth affair. If the Church listens humbly to what the scandals have revealed about its structures this time of tragedy and pain can also be a time of redemption. An American priest recently summed up what the child abuse scandals have occasioned his Church:

> It is my conviction that the pain we have been going through as a community and as a Church has been grace – painful grace, expensive grace, sometimes unwelcome grace – but grace that has come from a God who loves us enough to correct us and bring us to life again.

This experience can be valid for the Irish Church as well. The less defensive the Church is about its failures, the more open it is about its need to learn, the more able it will be to proclaim the Good News.

Kevin Hegarty
Kilmore Erris, County Mayo
April 1995

INTRODUCTION

The face of a serial paedophile priest suddenly fills television screens throughout Ireland and at the same time fills with fear the hearts of his prey. This image thrusts into their living-rooms unwelcome but haunting memories from their dark and secret pasts. The face in question is that of Fr Brendan Smyth, a Catholic priest, whose influence spread south from a prison cell in Northern Ireland, seeping slowly into the affairs of state of the Irish Republic, routing itself through the Attorney-General's office and the cabinet room, finally to bring down a government. Now it is an image which haunts an entire nation. The contemptuous swagger as he defiantly walked straight at the lens of an ITN camera seemed the hallmarks of a man who believed he was invincible, someone who thought he was above the law.

Close examination of the facts reveals why Fr Smyth had good reason for feeling this way. For more than four decades he had abused children in various parts of Ireland as well as in Scotland, Wales and the United States; during this time senior clergy within the Catholic Church in Ireland turned a blind eye to the activities of a criminal who used the robes of the Church as a cover for his perversion, and what began as a calamity for the Catholic Church ended in a national crisis. The television image of this priest became a central issue in the affairs of a state floundering to explain why it did not extradite Fr Smyth, and attempts to explain why Royal Ulster Constabulary (RUC) warrants lay unprocessed in the Attorney-General's office in Dublin for seven months produced unsatisfactory answers in the Irish Dáil (parliament).

At the end of a dramatic week in Irish politics, which saw the resignations of the Taoiseach and the newly appointed President of the High Court, there was an overwhelming sense of bewilderment in the corridors of power in Leinster House (Ireland's parliamentary building). There were few people in Ireland who did not believe that the Fr Smyth extradition affair once again raised questions about the special relationship between the Catholic Church and the state as defined in Article 44 of the Irish Constitution.

The finger of suspicion is directed towards the Catholic Church, for this is a story that many in the Catholic hierarchy did not want told, a story they did not want anyone to hear or read about, because of the shame its telling brings on those charged with the moral and spiritual leadership of Ireland's Catholic population.

By their own admission, even though they knew of Fr Smyth's propensity to molest children sexually from early in his religious life as a member of the Norbertine Community (and remember Fr Smyth joined the order in 1945) the order did not turn him over to the law: they simply moved him from one diocese to another, thus spreading suffering and fear over an even wider area. Twice they arranged transfers to America – and twice he offended there. Everywhere he went in his priestly garb he left behind a trail of misery – young lives put at risk of permanent blight by the dark touch of a paedophile.

In blunt terms, instead of caring for the abused, the Church authorities chose to shelter this criminal. In doing so, they surrendered the high moral ground they are presumed to occupy. The more they sheltered him, the more he sexually assaulted children who had the misfortune to trust him, not only as a priest, but as a family friend.

When official complaints were made about Fr Smyth, his order moved swiftly into action to persuade the family of the abused not to 'go public'. But when one Belfast family demanded his removal from circulation they were told the Norbertine Order could not accept responsibility for the movements of an adult, a man by now in his sixties, whose civil liberties would be eroded by any effort to curtail his movements, conveniently ignoring the fact that the Norbertine Abbot as Fr Smyth's religious superior had the power to assert disciplinary measures which might have had the effect of restricting the priest and reducing the likelihood of his continuing to abuse children. The family then tried to take the matter to a higher authority within the Church but when their cries for help seemed to be ignored by the spiritual leader of the faith in Ireland, Cardinal Cahal Daly, they could stand no more of what they took to be the Church's hypocrisy and so they turned elsewhere for help . . . they decided to go public. However, it did not stop Fr Smyth's allies in his order from attempting to continue the cover up. The family was approached by people from the priest's abbey to discuss the affair and to look for agreement not to go public with the charges, already laid before the forces of law and order. The family was horrified by this attempt to silence them: during the months immediately prior to their seeking the assistance of the police, members of the family had pleaded with the

Church for help but they were again ignored.

The cover-up attempts continued for the next three years as the priest left the jurisdiction of the RUC detectives who had interviewed and charged him on 8 March 1991. When the priest arrived at Grosvenor Road police station in Belfast that morning he had in his hand a small overnight bag. He clearly did not anticipate release that day but surprisingly, and against the best wishes of those who had interviewed him, bail was arranged. Promising to return when asked, Fr Smyth was given police bail of £100 on his own surety. He walked out of the police station at one o'clock that afternoon to return to his home in the Holy Trinity Abbey, Kilnacrott, Ballyjamesduff, County Cavan. It was to be three years before the RUC got sight of him again.

Once safely ensconced in the abbey, Fr Smyth refused to return to Northern Ireland to have papers relating to his preliminary enquiry served on him and for nine months he declined to take or return telephone calls from the police in Belfast. Instead he used the abbey to shelter from the law and throughout his more than two years on the run played a game of cat and mouse with the detectives by continuing to make secret trips back to Belfast to visit family friends.

Eventually, he was even able to defy legitimately served extradition papers, although as the extraordinary political developments in the Dáil revealed, in this he was unwittingly aided by the failure of the Irish Attorney-General's office to speedily process the extradition warrants.

It was not until 21 January 1994 – nearly four years

after the police in Northern Ireland began their investigation – that Fr Smyth finally travelled to Belfast to face a
court. His appearance in newspapers and on television that
day had police lines hot with new claims about his sexual
abuses and as a consequence the investigation was
widened to include new witnesses and new charges. The
extradition warrants contained nine charges but when Fr
Smyth was convicted in June 1994 he pleaded guilty to a
total of *seventeen* charges dating back to the 1960s. His
guilty pleas were the last hope the Church had that the
affair would go away quietly, given that the nature of the
pleas prevented a full ventilation of the facts in open
court. I have seen evidence of that view expressed in a
letter by a senior member of the Catholic hierarchy. What
the Church and its senior clerics had not bargained for
was the single-minded determination of those who had
suffered sexual abuse at the hands of the priest to make
the world aware it. They wanted the world to know the
truth the Church was so keen to conceal.

The abused found themselves in a strange situation:
they had stolen the high moral ground from the spiritual
guardians of the Catholic faith – their faith. By chance
their approach to me as a reporter for UTV's current
affairs programme, *Counterpoint*, made it the instrument
by which they would make the world aware of the crimes
perpetrated not only by Fr Smyth but by those charged
with responsibility for his discipline.

This then is a story of an investigation I conducted on
behalf of those who sought justice and truth. Without their
courage and encouragement it would not have been
possible to expose a wrong which powerful Churchmen

had succeeded in hiding for more than forty years. It chronicles the day the abused fought back against the abusers, the day they unburdened themselves of a guilt which had haunted them from childhood, and it was the act of individuals who felt wronged not once but twice by the Church. To the bitter end, all those in authority in the Catholic Church whom I approached singularly refused to be held accountable for Fr Smyth. This in itself was viewed by the accused and their families as an attempt to frustrate my investigation and to maintain the aloof attitude which up to this point had helped to protect Fr Smyth and therefore the Church from public accountability.

This is the story of Fr Brendan Smyth – a paedophile who sheltered, and who was allowed to shelter, behind the protective patronage of the Catholic Church in Ireland. Ultimately, his crimes not only shamed the Church, but brought down a government in circumstances heavy with suspicions of corruption and double-dealing.

It is dedicated to children everywhere who have suffered sexual abuse and who were encouraged to come forward after seeing those abused by Fr Smyth tell their stories on *Suffer Little Children*, the programme transmitted on 6 October 1994. This broadcast may forever have changed the face of Catholicism in Ireland and perhaps history will look kindly on it for having forced into the open the shameful deeds the Church for decades tried to bury.

Note: Throughout this book, the names of the abused and their families have been changed at their request to provide protection.

1

KILNACROTT

And tones that are tender, and tones that are gruff,
Are whispering over the sea,
Come back, Paddy Reilly, to Ballyjamesduff,
Come home, Paddy Reilly, to me.

Percy French

'Straight over the crossroads by the Percy French Hotel, two miles further on past the livestock mart; Kilnacrott is signposted, so just follow that road and you can't fail to see the abbey.' As I resumed my journey I could not help wondering if the young lad who had just given me directions to the Holy Trinity Abbey had any inkling of the secret which for over forty years had been hidden behind its walls.

This was my first visit to Ballyjamesduff, although the stretch of road from Clones to Cavan town was one which I first travelled twenty years before on the weekend Jimi Hendrix so tragically died. From that day, I have been fascinated by the crazy pattern the border draws between

North and South, between the state of Northern Ireland and the Irish Republic. One particular section of the road travellers zig-zag from one region to the other without any sign of a border checkpoint, policeman, soldier or customs officer. One moment in County Fermanagh, seconds later in County Cavan. You know when the switch happens because phone boxes change colour, traffic signs are different and the quality of road surface varies.

Ballyjamesduff – this was the place Percy French wanted Paddy Reilly to come back to: a small typically Irish rural town with wide streets and few road markings to interfere with the free movement of cars, vans, tractors and their trailers laden with livestock, foodstuffs and building materials. The dark skies and constant drizzle did nothing to flatter the appearance of the town made famous in the song and as I steered the white Subaru Legacy along the damp roadway leading out to the countryside, it seemed to me there was little here on a wet morning to make Paddy Reilly want to return.

A few miles past the signpost for Kilnacrott I came upon a large grey-and-white structure set well back in its own grounds but with nothing visible to indicate this was the abbey, certainly no obvious religious trappings. I parked at the gateway and pondered. To be frank the view from the roadway suggested a building which had long since surrendered its majesty to constant lashings from the inclement conditions. The emergence of a man dressed in the white robes of a monk settled the argument. I turned the ignition key and set off along the bumpy roadway which cut through a large grassy pasture. The monk in the white robes directed me to drive past the grey-and-white structure to the front of the building where I would find the reception area. I had apparently used the rear entrance. At the front there was a low modern building which appeared to grow out of the remains of an old stone edifice, clearly abandoned many years ago.

It was quiet as I walked through the double doors leading into a marble and stone entrance hallway where there was a display of religious articles: books, Mass cards, statues of Jesus and Mary, crucifixes and a magnificent display of candles of every conceivable size and colour, obviously to catch the attention of tourists. I had not come over a hundred miles to admire the abbey gift shop. I was here on business, on the trail of a priest who was a paedophile and who had for years, according to my sources, been guilty of systematically abusing children in Belfast. Two days earlier, on Saturday, 9 April 1994, I had spoken by telephone to the man responsible for running Kilnacrott Abbey, Abbot Kevin A. Smith, requesting an opportunity to interview him about his errant priest, Fr John Gerard 'Brendan' (his name in religion) Smyth. He asked me to make the request formally, in writing. The receptionist told me the Abbot was not immediately available so I handed in my letter and asked if I could look around the shop.

What I was hoping to find among the wide collection of pamphlets and books was a history of the religious order responsible for the running of this abbey, the Norbertines. I was out of luck and settled on the purchase of a few items which I thought might have a use when we began filming this story – a few candles and a statue of Jesus.

As the young woman in reception wrapped my goods, a priest dressed in the white robes of the order suddenly rushed in behind the counter to seize the statue from her. He moved swiftly to the doorway of the abbey chapel where he blessed my purchase and sprinkled it with holy water before returning to the counter to have it wrapped in brown paper.

Striking up a conversation as I waited for my change, the young priest inquired about my car outside. 'Is it a 1994 model?'

'No, it is two years old.'

'Has it been blessed?'

'No, it has not.'

He rushed off as the girl called me back over to the counter. By the time I had turned around to leave, the priest was waiting with a supply of holy water and a prayer-book and as he stepped ahead of me towards the doorway and my white Subaru, he asked if I was just passing through, so I explained my business. I was a reporter for Ulster Television and I had just delivered a letter to the Abbot concerning a member of the Norbertine Order, Fr Brendan Smyth. 'Do you know him?' I inquired. The priest did not respond to my question but having started on this mission, he continued to the car where he asked me to open the two doors on the driver's side as well as the boot.

The next few minutes passed by in something of a blur as he blessed the vehicle, doing his best to avoid any eye-contact with me. Indeed, the final moments of the blessing were conducted whilst he stood with his back to me so that he could quickly escape into the building once he had concluded this religious act. I was left standing alone to muse as to whether or not this blessing would bring me luck in my endeavours to track down a religious paedophile. [Five months later, I discovered that the young priest who had blessed my car, Fr Augustine Lane, died, on 10 July 1994, whilst on 'supply' to a church in England. Apparently he had taken his own life.]

As events were to unfold, the expression 'cover-up' would soon feature large in the telling of the Fr Smyth story. Meanwhile my thoughts were concentrated on what I had learned of the main character. It was clear that he was a traditionalist, someone who placed his trust in the old values of his faith and who was suspicious of the type of new thinking which was emerging within the ministry and among the people.

John Gerard Smyth was born in Belfast on 6 June 1927. He was raised in a terrace house off the Falls Road in West Belfast. Nansen Street is situated in an area populated mainly by Catholics and it was here he grew up and played as a child ... and it was in this environment that his life for the priesthood was mapped out. The young Smyth attended the Christian Brothers School at the bottom of the Falls Road – at Barrack Street, a few hundred yards from the city centre. The friendships cemented at school were to continue into adulthood ... and, as things turned out for some, the consequences will last a lifetime!

In 1945, at the age of eighteen, John Gerard Smyth left school and joined the Norbertine Order – a religious group within the wider Catholic Church family, also known as the Premonstratensians. The order was founded in the year 1120 (other authorities say 1119) at Prémontré in

France by St Norbert of Xanten, who intended it to blend the contemplative with active religious life. Nowadays life with the Norbertines is intensely liturgical with particular attention given to the Mass. Three special Masses are celebrated each day in every abbey; the *Missa Summa* (conventual Mass), a Mass in honour of the Blessed Virgin Mary and a Mass for dead confrères and benefactors.

My inquiries were to reveal a staggering truth about the operation of this religious order within the Catholic Church in Ireland. It appears to be entirely autonomous, answerable to no one else within the Church – not to the bishop of the diocese, much less to the All-Ireland Primate, Cardinal Cahal Daly in his role as the president of the Conference of Bishops. With a rank equivalent to that of bishop, Abbot Smith is the sole arbiter of disciplinary measures against members of the monastery of his order who step out of line. He may have to listen to what the Cardinal or a bishop has to say but he need not act upon such advice. Considering the influence of the Catholic Church in Ireland, it is nothing short of amazing that it tolerates religious orders where the Irish Church itself is not recognised as the authority. As we shall see, this is one of the factors which may have permitted the cover-up to continue for as long as it did.

As a novice, Fr Smyth was prepared for his religious life at Kilnacrott, the order's only abbey in Ireland, and two years after joining he was sent to Rome to study. He was an extremely bright and willing pupil and before returning to Ireland in 1951 he gained a degree in theology at the Gregorian University. According to a source in the Norbertine Community there was reason to suspect that by the time Fr Smyth returned from Italy, he had already misbehaved there. Although he did not become Fr Smyth's major religious superior until 1969 (Fr Brendan Smyth was subject to Fr Kevin Smith in the abbey during the years Fr Kevin was Prior – from 1959 onwards), Abbot Smith admitted that shortly after he began his religious life in 1945, 'his [Fr Brendan Smyth's] problem with children surfaced.'

Once back at Kilnacrott in 1951, it did not take Fr Smyth long to return to his sexual deviation. His cover for his actions was his apparent unlimited energy in making things happen around the abbey for children living in the Ballyjamesduff area. Fr Brendan was the new priest in the district and he soon secured the confidence of parents when he began organising catechism classes for children after Mass. He established a choir, trained altar boys for services in the abbey chapel. He did not confine himself to activities aimed at improving the religious stock of the community: he was instrumental in setting up May processions, Christmas parties and outings to the cinema. Naturally, his interest in the wellbeing of young people endeared him to parents, with whom he became as popular a figure as he was with some of the children.

Like so many others, before and since, Mary's parents thought Fr Smyth was the bee's knees – the best priest to ever come into their small rural community. They appreciated the religious discipline the priest had introduced to the lives of the children and, of course, the organisational skills he so effectively demonstrated. As Mary told the *Sunday Independent* (16 October 1994) she would be ordered by her parents: 'Get yourself up there now to devotions this evening.'

Mary was to discover Fr Smyth's secret soon enough: in 1952 when she was just eight years of age. The priest, then in his twenties, began systematically abusing her. His method of isolating children without raising the suspicions of their parents was to introduce the practice of 'punishments'. During Mass Fr Smyth would be watching, observing – even staring at the kids in the abbey chapel. He would be selecting one, two – maybe even three or four of them. The children knew exactly what was going on ... at least, they knew individually what he was up to. But because they never spoke a word about what happened in private with the priest, there was no collective knowledge, no strength in numbers; each one was extremely vulnerable and Fr Smyth exploited that fact.

During services, Fr Smyth would position himself among his confrères, just behind the altar. When it came to the catechism class, as he referred to it, he would say to whoever he had decided to single out, 'You were late', or 'You were talking during Mass'. Then the most dreaded words of all: 'You wait back.' Those selected would remain behind for their 'punishment'. They were 'reprimanded' in different rooms – boys in one, girls in another.

When he was with the boys, the altar servers, Mary said you could hear them getting a beating. They would be stripped first and then beaten. Their cries of pain echoed through the door and around the building. According to Mary, that sort of memory 'doesn't leave you'.

She recalled standing outside the door while he was with one of the other girls. As a member of the choir, Mary could easily be told to remain behind after the others had gone, and Fr Smyth would use the pretext that she had not been singing properly. When she went into the room alone with the priest, he would pull her close to him and explain what he thought she had done wrong. Avoiding his eyes was not always easy but it was the aim of individuals like Mary. Either way, she would soon find herself on his knee but it clearly was not the same as sitting on her father's knee; her daddy did not have this strange hard feeling, is how Mary explained it. Unlike Fr Smyth's her daddy's hands did not gradually creep up her leg, under her outer clothing and eventually beneath her underwear. As innocence was lost the priest would angrily rebuke any child who dared turn to look at his face. 'Don't look at me,' he would bark. 'Look away.' For years Mary, like so many others before and since, had to endure his constant 'touching', his hands wandering up her skirt until he touched her genital area.

The worst moment for Mary was the day Fr Smyth made her strip off completely. She cried; he gave her sweets – he always had a plentiful supply of sweeties about his person – and then he sent her home. She was in tears as she fled the room, passing the next girl waiting in line as she rushed for the fresh open air. On this day, Mary cried more than ever before but by the time she walked home the tears had dried up. She kept her secret, his secret. What Mary could not have known is that during all the years Fr Smyth was abusing her and others inside Kilnacrott Abbey, he was also extremely active beyond the boundaries of Ballyjamesduff. Even in the lean '50s of post-war Europe, Fr Smyth somehow managed to run a car, his means of regularly making the same journey I was now making northwards, crossing the border into Northern Ireland.

Fr Brendan Smyth would have known this route so well, but he had also experienced life well beyond these shores. I was thinking of the United States; just over a week earlier I had returned from there, from temperatures twenty below freezing in North Dakota, eleven miles from the United States-Canada border. I'd gone there after meeting in Belfast families of those who had been abused by Smyth, some of whom realised he was in the United States because of the Christmas cards he had sent back to friends in Ireland.

In order to trace the priest's exact location there without alerting the Catholic Church in Ireland to my interest in him, I had contacted the Catholic press office in England. Time enough to contact the Irish Catholic press office when I knew more about the case, when I had built up a more complete file on the movements and activities of Fr Smyth.

On the journey back to Belfast, I thought about how I had become involved in the story of the paedophile priest, back to the day I received a telephone call from Sally.

2

IN THE BEGINNING . . .

I feel now even after all this time, I have a duty and a moral responsibility to speak out and make people aware of what has happened in order that it won't happen again. If I had spoken out and told somebody in the seventies, then what happened to these children after me would not have happened and something could have been done at the time to stop him in his tracks.

Sally, abused by Fr Brendan Smyth for about five years during the '70s, speaking on 22 February 1994.

Sally was serving tea when it happened. As the children gathered around the table, her boyfriend ushering them to the dining-room, the little portable television set in the kitchen showed the face of a child sex molester walking into court. In the second or so it took her to recognise the man, Sally knew her life could never again be the same. For this was the priest her family had regarded as a friend during her formative childhood years and it was the face of a man she'd grown to despise . . . it was the face of her abuser. Sally watched and listened as she heard the charges against Fr Brendan Smyth. In her state of shock, the exact details did not really register. She gleaned enough to know that finally the priest was being exposed publicly as a sex offender. The delight of witnessing his obvious discomfort was tempered by other, decidedly unpleasant thoughts, about the personal ramifications of this unexpected television appearance by Fr Smyth.

Painful memories of her secret past invaded her consciousness; her mind was reeling, joy one moment, stabbing pain the next. Hysteria stirred inside her; it was a battle to contain it. Her conscience told her the time had come finally to reveal the secrets she had concealed for so many years. Now in her thirties, Sally had already suffered the break-up of her marriage. She lived with Robert and the children of that marriage. Tears ran down her cheeks as Robert moved to her side; she had to tell him.

The evening meal was eaten in a strange silence. The children sensed something had upset mummy but they did not pursue the reasons for it. It was only after the dishes had been washed and the kids were tucked up in bed that she finally spoke of the pain she had suffered more than twenty years earlier. Robert listened intently as Sally sobbed her way through her tale of the abuse. By the end of that evening of 21 January 1994, Sally and Robert agreed she would contact a solicitor next day before going to the police officers investigating the case.

Next morning, instead of going to her civil service

office, Sally made the short bus journey into the city centre to keep the appointment with her solicitor she had made by telephone first thing that morning. Within twenty-four hours of seeing the face she had grown to hate, she had unburdened herself in a lengthy statement about her experiences. Then she went to the police and offered the investigating detectives the benefit of her knowledge of Fr Brendan Smyth. By the time Sally had provided the police with vital information about the *modus operandi* of the priest, the pain of the memories had turned into anger, anger that she had allowed herself to conceal the truth about Fr Smyth's activities for so long. For the first time in her life, Sally realised she had an important role to play in ensuring that Fr Smyth could never again injure children.

But as if to guarantee that Fr Smyth would not escape justice or at the very least public admonishment on this occasion, Sally took one other step in the next weeks: she contacted me in the *Counterpoint* office at UTV. A few weeks earlier, by chance, I'd met her boyfriend Robert at a small club in Belfast, where we had exchanged business cards in relation to a story about another matter entirely.

I was invited to Sally's home to hear her story, to arrive when the children had been put to bed. She sought assurances about protection of her identity and it was only after a half-hour of talking about how this should be achieved that she spoke about her childhood in West Belfast. What she had to say that bitterly cold February night was in itself chilling.

Brought up in a stable family environment, Sally's difficulties with Fr Smyth coincided with the beginning of the civil disturbances so evident in streets not far from her home. For the people living in her street the only visible sign of what were to become known as 'the Troubles' were the occasional foot-patrols of British soldiers. Sally thinks she was lucky to live in one of the better housing areas of West Belfast.

It was a happy home, a pleasant environment for developing minds, a place where Sally and her sister were content in a way only children who are protected from the evils of the big bad world outside the home can be. Everything was fine until the day Fr Brendan Smyth entered their world and for the first time in their lives there was a breach in the protection provided by their parents. Fr Smyth was introduced to Sally's parents by one of her uncles, who had attended the same school as the priest when they both lived in the Falls Road area.

Of course, it may not just have been a coincidence that Fr Smyth started visiting Sally's home; there was certainly an attraction there for a paedophile with a preference for children from the age of six to twelve. In any event, having a priest call regularly at the house was considered by Catholic families as something of an honour and so for Sally's parents the arrival of Fr Smyth was a blessing. When the priest showed very obvious signs of taking a special interest in the children that was a bonus. No Catholic parent would have any suspicion about a priest who just happened to have a knack of getting on with the kids.

At first, Fr Smyth's attentions to Sally and her sister were viewed as nothing more than affection from a man with a genuine love and regard for children. Furthermore,

Sally's was not the only house in the street to be blessed with visits from the Norbertine priest. It was the same in every home he visited – there were children, and he always displayed a special skill in getting them to play along with his games . . . grabbing and tickling, turning them upside down so the girls' knickers showed and pulling them up on to his knee where he could hold them close to him. Parents constantly witnessed this pattern of behaviour. They were just delighted he was showering so much attention on the kids.

Sally remembers summer days sitting on the step outside her house, playing with friends. As in any urban area, children used their gardens and the street as their playgrounds. But when Fr Smyth drove up, all the playing children would break off the game, whatever it was, to rush to the priest's car. To Sally, he was like the Pied Piper or Santa Claus. The boot of his car was always loaded with sweets. Sweets of all kinds. The kids would be hopping, skipping and jumping all around him looking for his favours. Money never seemed to be one of Fr Smyth's problems. But the priest's speciality was to begin to programme the children for sexual contacts right under the noses of their parents. It was here during his 'tickling' sessions or when he was fooling around at horseplay that his hands would begin to wander and then linger on a bare leg or around their bottoms. Of course his 'tickling' technique varied according to whether parents were about or not. He knew how to be careful, how to avoid arousing their suspicions. If they were not around, then his hands would advance up a girl's skirt to the top of her thigh where his fingers would seek out her underwear. Boys might find his hand slipping down the back of their trousers inside their underwear, fingers nipping their backsides. He would be more cautious when parents were around, but their presence did not mean Fr Smyth could resist going just as far as he reckoned he could get away with undetected. One way of isolating children from their parents was to offer to take them away for runs in his car. Sally remembers very clearly the day-trip along the Antrim coast he organised in 1970 for her and her sister.

On the journey north he actually stopped the car and got into the rear seat with the sisters to engage in a bit of 'tickling' which the girls had to endure but truthfully did not really enjoy or understand. After reaching their destination the priest took the girls to see an aunt before taking them to an hotel along the coast for tea. Again, money was no object as they enjoyed this treat before the long journey home to Belfast. Up until now it had been a pleasant day out and Sally was quite relaxed.

On the return journey she became really upset. She was ten years old at the time, her sister just eight, and as they set off for home, Fr Smyth made the eight-year-old sit in the front passenger seat. Sally did not like being separated but as the car made its way along the coast, her sister was laughing and giggling as the priest continued his apparent affection. Then things went horribly wrong. The laughing and giggling turned at first to frowns; then a look of panic was followed by fear. Sally could see that her sister was in some distress. Tears soon followed. Sally got the priest to allow her sister back into the rear seat of the car so that at least she could offer some comfort. It was some days after they got back home before Sally learned that the priest had tried to sexually molest her sister. The eight-year-old had informed her parents: 'He tried to put his finger in my hole.'

From this point onwards the family's attitude towards Fr Smyth changed dramatically, Sally's memory was that of a child listening in on adult conversations. She did not know exactly what was going on but something had definitely happened. Her mother's attitude to their visitor cooled and there was a row in the house when her father challenged the priest's credibility. The result was that Fr Smyth stopped calling at the house when Sally's mother was there. She believes he was told not to return to the house. Sally's parents were alarmed and horrified by what their eight-year-old daughter had told them. But Fr Smyth was not that easily deterred: for some years after this edict from the parents, he continued to call at the house when they were not around. He sneaked into the house when he knew both were at work and when he knew Sally, as the elder, was in charge of her sister.

In spite of the discomfort which seemed to increase with every sighting of the priest, Sally's upbringing prevented her from being rude. Even when he called at the house while she was on her own, she made him cups of tea. That's how she had been brought up. You were kind to visitors. Her reward from Fr Smyth was further abuse.

Although Sally dreaded these moments, she did not inform her parents of the feelings of dislike she experienced every time she saw the priest. She began to feel decidedly uncomfortable when he was around, especially when he began asking her for kisses. The first time he wanted a kiss, Sally offered her cheek on the basis that the priest wanted only to give her a peck of affection but she was horrified when he turned her head round to face him so he could kiss her on the lips. One day she tried to wriggle free of him as he put her on his knee and he grabbed her tightly. When she made it clear he was hurting her, the priest calmly told her that if she stopped struggling to get free, she would not get hurt.

Worse still, Fr Smyth started turning up at Sally's school, the Cross and Passion on the Glen Road in West Belfast. Somehow he managed to persuade the nuns in charge that he needed to see Sally privately. Sally resented being brought to him and left alone in a room with him. When this had occurred on three separate occasions she decided enough was enough... and she bluntly informed the priest of this. He had asked her to come into the room and close the door but she stood defiantly, arms folded, in the doorway. No, she told him. She did not enjoy his touches up her skirt, around her breasts, and she certainly did not like his last attempt to kiss her on the mouth.

Even at the time she stood in the doorway at the age of fourteen, almost trembling with fear at her own defiance, Sally had not told one single person about the assaults on her body by the priest. She could not bring herself to tell her parents, her teachers, her friends, because she did not think anyone would believe her. Having a priest as a family friend was an honour. Telling about his perverted ways would bring dishonour on her and her family. Fr Smyth was his usual bright, friendly self. He asked Sally to come on into the room: he had sweets and wanted her to sit on his knee. He asked how she was, how were things going. She said she was all right where she was, crushing the fright and nervousness that were welling up inside and finding a new strength to ignore the priest's command. She worried, thinking she would be 'killed' for this act of treachery, but he seemed to sense she was at last putting up barriers and so he did not force the issue. Sally seized the opportunity with both hands and said goodbye.

She'd been in the room with the priest for just under five minutes and as she left to return to class one of the nuns asked how she knew Fr Smyth. Sally simply replied that he was a friend of the family but the resolve that she had found within herself that day helped her tell the nun that she did not want to be taken out of class again to see the priest as it held her back with her work. That was the last day she ever saw Fr Smyth at her school. The year was 1974 and it was to be nearly twenty years before Sally realised the full extent of the damage Fr Smyth had caused, before she learned that he had also abused some of her friends, next-door neighbours and even some of her relatives.

By the time I left Sally's home that night, I was beginning to understand what Sally meant on the day she first spoke to me on the phone when she said this story was 'dynamite'. She agreed to do an interview for our television programme and she promised to speak to the others who had been abused by Fr Smyth – those people with whom she'd renewed her friendships with in the few troubled days since Fr Smyth's image first appeared on her portable television in the kitchen. Sally was the first link in a chain which would eventually lead to the damning revelations. I did not even begin to appreciate as I said goodnight to Sally the full extent of the story which was about to unfold!

3

BETRAYAL OF TRUST

The Catholic Church is accountable for its members and I think they would have to have a very serious look at the behaviour of priests in future. I know it's very difficult for a priest now to go into a home and touch a child. I mean, that is something that is very unfortunate but people need to build up faith again. And the Church would need to have a very good look at what is happening. Smyth might be an isolated case but I do not know what the future holds but in our case the Church has been absolutely no help whatsoever and I find that very sad because to me there's a law for Church members and a law for their parishioners or for members of their flock.

Seamus, father of four children abused by Fr Smyth, speaking shortly before the priest was jailed at Belfast Crown Court.

From the very first moment we met, I knew Bernie was one of life's achievers, someone who would refuse to take no for an answer – a mother of four children who had all been subjected to Fr Smyth's perverted behaviour, who was to become a priceless asset in the pursuit of the truth; her determination to wrestle justice out of betrayal and mistrust an essential tool in digging for facts.

Stung by the lack of assistance from the Catholic Church, she and her husband Seamus were now prepared to throw their weight behind any activity that would expose the continuing cover-up within a section of the Church. They were disgusted by the attitude of the local parish when they made approaches for help and as far as they were concerned the Church had turned its back on them in their hour of need. When Seamus went to the local parochial house to inform their parish priest what had been happening to his children, there was not so much as a telephone call in response, never mind a house call. The couple had hoped to get some support, perhaps someone to come and talk to the children, to offer something, practical and/or spiritual, to guide them through what was the most painful experience ever to happen the family. Seamus says he made it clear to the local priest that he realised that the case may well have been a one-off, and he was not going to allow this to dispose him to tar all priests with the same brush. Indeed, in his experience as someone baptised and reared as a Catholic, he had found most priests genuine and caring.

Sally had put me in touch with Bernie and Seamus and when I first met them in their home in West Belfast in February 1994, I discovered that no one in the house was attending Mass. The facts of their case make it easy to understand why they no longer practise their faith. The story of Bernie and Seamus, more than any other, epitomises the depths to which Fr Brendan Smyth was prepared to sink.

It was in the early 1950s that Bernie first met the priest. He was then in his mid-twenties. Even in these early days of his religious life, he could afford a car and made regular journeys from County Cavan to his old childhood haunts on the Falls Road. Visiting the side-streets off the Falls, he would sign Mass cards to supplement his income and at the same time he was in a position to bring over the border the odd couple of pounds of butter which were in more plentiful supply down south. On the way back to the abbey at Ballyjamesduff, he would buy supplies of electrical goods to smuggle into the Republic. And, of course, while he was in Belfast the old school friends he visited were prepared to slip him a pound here and there.

Bernie remembers the priest calling at her mother's house in West Belfast and that her parents regarded it an honour to have a priest call regularly. Fr Smyth watched Bernie grow up, met her friends and eventually her boyfriends, and when Seamus and Bernie decided to get married, it was Fr Smyth who performed the wedding service, as a wedding gift, he said. There was a bond of friendship which lasted many, many years as Fr Smyth honoured Bernie and Seamus too with his presence in their new home.

The only reason Seamus knew Fr Smyth was because of the connections with Bernie's family. He enjoyed the hours he spent in conversation with the priest, chatting about politics, theology and travel, particularly about his adventures in the United States. In politics, the priest leaned towards the republican viewpoint but according to Seamus, he could make an intelligent argument on any of the topics they discussed as they whiled away many a pleasant hour in the midst of great political upheaval in West Belfast. The priest shared Seamus's interest in cars. He drove thousands of miles in the year and according to Seamus, he would change the car every year or so, because of the high mileage. Fr Smyth watched Seamus and Bernie's four children grow up. He was always there to play with them, bring them sweeties or take them away for trips in his car, sometimes overnight journeys to Dublin and beyond. He was always welcome in their home.

Then it all began to fall apart as they started to learn the truth about the priest who had been part of their lives from the very first moment they'd met. In November 1988 Bernie and Seamus had a visitor who had been a very close friend of the family right from the 1950s. This young man, let us call him Anthony, had lived in the same street as Sally and, like Sally, his parents befriended the priest from Kilnacrott Abbey, offering him the freedom to come and go as he pleased and occasionally giving the young cleric presents of money. Now in 1988 the young man was distraught; for years he had carried the burden of Fr Smyth's sexual assaults on him without telling anyone. It became a major problem when he got married and there is no doubt in his mind that it was the major factor in the break-up of his marriage.

Anthony asked if Bernie and Seamus could help him by providing their home as a venue for a confrontation with Fr Smyth and they were happy to oblige. The occasion chosen was the confirmation of one of their own children. Anthony shocked them with his story of sexual abuse by Fr Smyth going back almost thirty years to when he was a child of six. The confrontation took place as planned, with Bernie and Seamus by agreement out of the house at the moment Anthony challenged the priest about the years of sexual abuse he had been forced to endure. When Fr Smyth learned that Anthony was now attending counselling, he even suggested that he too should go to the same therapist but this was a offer which Anthony felt no difficulty refusing. It was, incidentally, the last time Fr Smyth ever entered Bernie's home. Bernie and Seamus have not spoken to him since that day in February 1989.

Anthony's nightmare of abuse lasted for many years, right up into his early teens, and he was beginning to wonder if his brothers or other young people had been interfered with in the same way. By the time he came to see Bernie and Seamus he had already discovered that his younger brother John had also been abused throughout the sixties and seventies. It was not easy to find the courage to face close friends and relatives to tell them about this, that the priest they so respected and admired was a criminal with, apparently, no remorse for the dreadful activities he engaged in with the children of his former school friends.

In Seamus and Bernie's home, Anthony quietly told them about his experiences. They sat in wonder at his tale of suffering. They were horrified and devastated to hear how devious Fr Smyth had been over the years he was sexually abusing Anthony. Then came the dreaded moment when Anthony asked his friends if they had noticed any abnormal behaviour from their kids when Fr Smyth was around.

This is where the lives of this hard-working couple began to fray at the edges; this was the beginning of a nightmare which persists to this day and will, in all probability, stay with them forever. They were devastated by Anthony's tale of corruption. What made matters even worse was the realisation that there had been odd behaviour on the part of their children in the past which they had put down to childish notions. Now, with the benefit of hindsight they saw that certain behaviour patterns tended to coincide with visits of Fr Smyth.

Bernie and Seamus felt that night that something in their lives was lost for ever. Almost immediately recriminations began; a dreadful feeling of guilt overwhelmed them. Had they really missed something obvious? Had they let their children down? How could Fr Smyth have done this to them? They recalled edgy reactions in their kids at the first sign of Fr Smyth in the street outside. They would bolt out the back of the house or snuggle into a seat beside their parents. The parents put this down to the childish games and pranks the priest played but now as Anthony opened his heart to them they realised there was probably a sinister side to it. Their children had not yet confirmed any of this information to them. This task lay ahead. And it took many months before they could bring themselves to chat to the kids. Fr Smyth was not around; after the confrontation with Anthony he tended to make himself scarce around those homes in West Belfast where Anthony's friends lived. For months Bernie and Seamus contemplated their next move, not pushing the kids too hard and not wishing to intrude on their suffering. However everyone in the family realised that the issue of Fr Brendan Smyth would have to be confronted very soon.

Christmas 1988 was not the usual happy family affair. Bernie and Seamus had a lot on their minds as they watched the kids open their presents on Christmas morning. Their stomachs churned at the thought of what these innocents had suffered at the hands of the man they had revered, that their children were concealing hideous pain inflicted by this priest.

This nagging pain has not left them and for Seamus, the suffering has found expression in writing. This poem illustrates the inner feelings of someone who feels betrayed. It comes from the depths of a man riddled with anger one moment, with misplaced guilt the next, and a deep bewilderment about the sordid actions of the priest whose company he so enjoyed over the years.

Victim of a Child Sex Abuser

To the young and innocent he must come,
On his face a disarming smile,
But evil in his heart.
Yet he bore no sign to tell of his intent.
The young warm body was his need;
Its personal privacy his desire.
Boy or girl, he did not care,
The feelings should be the same,
As long as they were young, innocent and available.
Victims were sought far and wide,
In places where he would feel secure
To use his hands on children
Who did not know the meaning of his sickly smile.

The first caress would be a start,
From which his heart would race,
And feelings of pleasure would engulf

His evil being to say, this feels good,
Next time I will feel a little more.
The first touch, I thought, an accident?
His hands so sure and quick.
About the second I was not so sure
But the third and the fourth
Scramble my thoughts while my body tingled.
Was this right or was it wrong?
My scrambled thoughts would ask.
I did not know. I was too young to understand
That, however pleasant, evil deeds were being done.
My troubled thoughts would often ask,
What could I do? Who would believe me?
No one, he said, would believe me.
With my innocence gone, I was seriously troubled.

Many long years have passed,
And still I do not feel free from all the attention
That he gave me.
God, would I ever feel free
From the horrors of my childhood.
We are told, you said, we should forgive and forget,
I am sorry, God: that I cannot do.
The abuser was one of your representatives;
Because of this, I trusted him,
Now, I wonder, do you really care?

Now as I sat sipping a cup of midday coffee with Bernie
and Seamus, I was struck by the sincerity of a couple who
in the face of adversity could still smile and crack jokes.
From the outset they wanted me to know that their story,

if I was to be permitted to tell it, must not be told in an insensitive manner, in a salacious way. They knew that Fr Smyth had been offending for many years. They also believed that this must have been known to his immediate superiors. However they did not believe that the Norbertine Order or the hierarchy were prepared to take whatever steps were necessary to ensure that Fr Smyth was punished and that he did not have the opportunity to re-offend. I knew from the conversation that they had no real desire to have me hear their story. If another way could have been found to heal the betrayal they had suffered, that is the route they would have taken. I was left in no doubt that the only reason I was in their home was that, in their view, publicly describing their pain was their only recourse. Had the Church taken the time at least to sympathise with the family, to offer some kind of tangible assistance in their hour of need, Bernie and Seamus would not be sitting with me in their living-room speaking about the dreadful hurt done to their children and, of course, to themselves.

Shortly after Anthony had revealed Fr Smyth's secret life as a paedophile Bernie and Seamus very gingerly broached the subject of sex abuse with their children, full of trepidation at the very thought of it. It is not the kind of situation parents are prepared for, not the kind of thing you do every day.

For Bernie, it was an ordeal: she discovered that on several occasions while she was in the kitchen preparing a meal, Fr Smyth was in the living-room sexually assaulting her children. If someone had tried to suggest such a thing in the past, she would have regarded him or her as a liar. But this, unfortunately, was no lie: this was the sad, sordid truth about betrayal. As they listened to their children recount their tales about Fr Smyth, the couple were moved to tears. Seamus thought about the abuse of trust by the priest and could not help feeling that perhaps there never was any value in the friendship he thought he shared with Fr Smyth, that perhaps the only reason for the frequent visits from the cleric was access to the children in the house.

For over twelve months Bernie and Seamus lived their lives in a maelstrom of emotions: anger, frustration, hurt, pain and worst of all the inability to see clearly enough to make the next move. That decision was effectively made for them in February, 1990 when Susan, one of their daughters, was speaking to a social worker at the offices of the Catholic Family Welfare Society in Belfast. She had reason to speak to someone about a totally unrelated matter and in the course of her conversation revealed to the startled social worker that she had suffered sex abuse in childhood and that her abuser was a priest by the name of Brendan Smyth. This meeting on 23 February was historic for it represented the beginning of the end of Fr Brendan Smyth's life as a child sex abuser. The social worker advised Bernie that according to law, the police would have to be informed and thus the decision about what to do next was taken for Bernie and Seamus. The family doctor was contacted so that counselling sessions for the children could begin immediately. Once the police were informed, they too would have to see the children but before that happened the parents had an opportunity to speak to the police about how they would proceed with the case. Bernie and Seamus arranged to meet the female sergeant who would initially take charge of the inquiry on 2 March 1990.

Statistically, Susan became one of the thousand cases of child sex abuse reported every year in the greater Belfast area, of which less than half end up in the courts. When an allegation of abuse is made it is not just the police who move into action. There is a special process involving social services in a joint investigation and by the time detectives actually meet the individual making the allegations quite a bit of ground work has been done into the accuser's background, the family and the suspected perpetrator. Younger children are taken to the RUC's Child Care Unit, a purpose-built bungalow located inside a Belfast police station, where the child is made to feel as comfortable as possible away from the more intimidating atmosphere of a police interview room. It is here that the police and social services have specially trained officers to conduct an interview with the principal objective of gathering what Sergeant William McAuley describes as 'evidence at its best quality'. It is not that children are any less believable than adults but when it comes to a criminal court case, the child's evidence must be presented in the way that shows honesty and validity. Great care must be taken to search out as much corroborating evidence as possible, checking with other witnesses to ensure that the child's description of times, dates and whereabouts tally. The Child Care Unit is also fitted with specialised medical equipment under the control of forensic medical officers who try to uncover uncontaminated evidence to back up the statements made by the accuser. In many cases where the allegations are not made until some years after the abuses have taken place, there is no hope of finding this quality of forensic evidence and so it is down to good old-fashioned detective work and interviewing technique to substantiate the allegations by means of corroborating statements or by confessions from the accused. Such was the case for the children of Bernie and Seamus.

From the outset, Bernie and Seamus were reassured by the manner of the police officer that their case would be thoroughly investigated and that, most important of all, the investigation would be conducted sensitively with the children's best interests as the priority. It was agreed that a local health board office would be a more suitable venue for the first meeting between the children and police. On 7 March the social worker called at Bernie and Seamus's house and with the family packed into two cars the children were driven to the appointed place to begin playing their part. It was here that specially trained police officers gently persuaded the kids to talk aloud of their experiences and of the nightmare that followed. It was here that the police began to build up a picture of the paedophile priest. As far as Bernie and Seamus were concerned, at last someone was prepared to listen to their story and to take seriously the allegations of sexual misconduct against the priest with a view to preventing his hurting more children.

The greatest challenge for investigators is to satisfy themselves that children tell the truth and that they do it in such a way as to give the prosecution the best possible evidence to proceed to court. Notes were carefully taken of times, dates and places: as much detail as the children could remember, given that they were searching their memories for details of events going back a good many years. Bernie and Seamus were deeply impressed by the demeanour of the police officers, by the care and sympathy shown to the children as they relived the horrors of the past. They were not themselves present during the interviews as they thought their presence might inhibit the kids.

As he learned more about the priest's ability to carry out these assaults under the very noses of the parents, Seamus realised just how much Fr Smyth used his intelligence to get away with his crimes. He recalled occasions when the children were in their bedrooms with flu or a toothache and how the priest was allowed to go up there and spend time alone with them. Bernie and Seamus brought their children up to enjoy some privacy when in their own rooms. That attitude still obtains, as Seamus candidly admits that as long as the children are receiving proper counselling to help them rebuild shattered lives, neither he nor Bernie need ever push them into revealing to them all the details of the abuses. They thought the children's first visit to the police, on 7 March 1990, would bring a swift conclusion to the whole affair and allow them all to try to get on with their lives.

I spent several hours in their home that first day as Bernie and Seamus gave me a detailed account of their experiences. By the time I left I had begun to understand the magnitude of the story and the reason for their feeling of utter frustration. I came away with an overwhelming admiration for the fortitude of individuals bonded together in a family prepared to face adversity as one. It was here, in a Catholic home in West Belfast, that the words cover-up were first used . . . the cover-up that was to be exposed in the coming months, showing that over a period of many years, a number of individuals within the Norbertine Order knew of Fr Smyth's paedophilia but chose not to use the law to deal with the problem.

4

BACK TO SCHOOL

As far as we were concerned that was the end of it – in 1971. Surely somebody should have taken steps to stop him doing exactly what he has been able to do all along, which is totally disgusting. It's horrifying that the church would let a priest continue to mingle with young people which he obviously did, because he has been linked with molesting children right up to 1988. I think it is disgusting; my parents think it is totally disgusting.

Sarah, (abused by Fr Smyth in a Catholic school in 1971) speaking in 1994. She complained; her parents complained to the school and were promised Fr Smyth would be stopped.

I left Bernie and Seamus thinking about whether or not they would appear in our programme and made arrangements to approach Anthony, his brother John and Bernie's daughter Susan, to see if they would talk to me. It was time for me to go back to Sally. She had been responsible for first asking Bernie and Seamus about meeting me and was now busy trying to find out if another girl, Sarah, would tell me her story. Judging by what I had learned already from Sally, this story was vitally important if I was to present the full historical perspective on Fr Smyth's activities. It was alleged that Sarah was targeted for abuse at her school as far back as 1971, when her official complaint to the school authorities had brought a promise to her parents that they would deal with the wayward priest. Sarah had grown up in the same West Belfast street as Sally and Anthony and his brother John. She knew Bernie and Seamus's daughter Susan through her friendship with Anthony and John. They'd played together as children, and together they accepted Fr Smyth's money and sweets. They did not know at the time that he was singling each of them out for his sexual activities.

At this stage I was still gathering information, still finding out the extent of the abuses inflicted by the priest in order to establish his *modus operandi* before making an official approach to the Church. Sarah confirmed the story when I telephoned to ask for a meeting and I was delighted when she agreed to see me at her home. Like Sally, Sarah was living with her two children, Sean and Mairead, was separated from her husband and, like Sally she worked in the civil service. On the first occasion I drove to her home in a tree-lined street in South Belfast, I met the children, both fanatical supporters of Liverpool football club – a fact which spiced up the early conversation as I am an avid Manchester United supporter. I sparred with the two Liverpool supporters and assured them that their team was not going to win anything this season and that United were on course for a remarkable treble of the Littlewoods Cup, the FA Cup and the Premier League title they had won the previous season for the first time in twenty-six years. The children were charming and well-mannered but had the confidence to engage in conversation in an adult way, making it obvious that they were quite familiar with the social graces required when visitors called. They were certainly giving as good as they got, convinced that Liverpool were in a period of transition and that very soon they would be back to form, sure to win the league title and the European Cup. Sarah put an end to our argument, cajoling the children towards the stairs and bed. Sarah's sister Averil was there and remained once the children had gone as Sarah gently grilled me to discover just how much I knew about Fr Smyth's activities. She made it clear she had no objection to telling me everything she could but was adamant that she did not want to be identified or to appear in any disguised shape or form on the television programme.

A bottle of chilled white wine, Chablis I think, was produced from the fridge and we settled down for a lengthy chat. Sarah's father had gone to school with Fr Smyth in West Belfast and the priest was a guest at her parents' wedding. Sarah did not remember the priest's calling very often to the house when she was young: once in a blue moon was how she put it, but the frequency of his visits increased when she began attending St Dominic's High School on the Falls Road in Belfast in 1969.

Of course it is only now with the benefit of hindsight that Fr Smyth's sudden interest in renewing his friendship with Sarah's family became explicable: Sarah was at an age which suited his sexual craving. Just as with Sally at the Cross and Passion School, it appears that Fr Smyth could call at her school and ask the nuns in charge if a pupil could be fetched from class to a room where he could spend time alone with her. It happened with Sarah at St Dominic's on three occasions. The priest had not been seen for a few years when he turned up unexpectedly at the school where he apparently told the nuns he was a family friend of Sarah and that the family had said he could call into the school from time to time to see the girl. But on this day Sarah had friends waiting so she spent very little time in the room, what Sarah described as 'a guest room, a beautiful drawing-room', to which the priest had been shown when he arrived at the school. Fr Smyth told Sarah to tell her parents he was asking for them and she left.

However, things were not so straightforward on the second occasion the priest arrived at St Dominic's. This time Sarah was fetched from class during a lesson and brought into the drawing-room, where she was left alone with the priest. He put her on his knee and began holding her very close. Nothing else happened on this occasion except, as Sarah recalls, a few questions from Fr Smyth about boyfriends. His third visit was a frightening experience for the thirteen-year-old Sarah because this time when she arrived at the room, he took her inside and locked the door before setting her on his knee. Sarah described his behaviour on this third occasion as 'touchy', meaning that the priest was touching her more and she was compelled to elbow him to get him to take his hand down out from under her skirt and her underwear. Summoning up all her courage, Sarah says she pushed the priest away to get back to her class, but she could not hold back tears when she met a friend out in the corridor as she fled from the room. She spat out her story about the interfering priest just as Sr Joan, one of the sisters in the school, rounded a corner to witness her very obvious distress.

Sarah says it was her friend who blurted out to the inquiring nun exactly what she'd been told a few moments earlier. The headmistress, Sr Virgilius, was contacted and asked Sarah to repeat her tale about the priest before suggesting that she go home immediately and inform her parents of the day's events. More tears as she explained to the school principal that Fr Smyth was a family friend and it would be difficult to inform her parents. Sr Virgilius suggested, according to Sarah, that her friend accompany her home so that there would be some support for her when she told her parents. The two girls set off for Sarah's home to break the news. Sarah's mother was outraged and immediately telephoned her husband at work and from this point on, the matter was taken out of Sarah's hands. Her mother and father began taking steps to prevent the priest from coming into their lives ever again. Sarah says there were telephone calls between the principal, Sr Virgilius, and her mother and father. Sarah heard one side of some of these conversations and was told enough to calm her down and reassure her that the priest would not be back in her life.

Sarah says her parents were assured by Sr Virgilius that Fr Smyth would never again darken the doors of the school, and that the Church would take steps to ensure this. Sarah says her father was told that the incident would be referred to a higher Church authority and he agreed not to proceed any further with the matter. When Fr Smyth later sent Sarah a Mass card for her birthday, her father got in touch with the priest personally to tell him not to contact anyone in the family ever again . . . and that, they thought was the end of the whole affair.

It all resurfaced, however, in 1994, when Sarah and her family saw, with the same surprise as Sally, shots of the priest going into a Belfast court. When they made inquiries about who was responsible for bringing the charges, they were stunned to discover it was their former next-door neighbours. Sarah's father was shocked and angered to discover that Fr Smyth had been allowed to continue his abuses against children in Belfast right up to the late 1980s, so outraged in fact, that he telephoned St Dominic's to speak to Sr Virgilius. He rang on two separate occasions, first on a Friday and then next morning, and spoke to two different people but the message from each was the same: Sr Virgilius was dead. Disappointed with the response from the school and unable to speak to the former principal, Sarah's father gave up at this stage. Sarah, however, did not, and again, like Sally, she approached the police to provide more evidence to help put the priest behind bars. As the police investigation was given that new impetus in January 1994, I was about to make a couple of startling discoveries about St Dominic's and Sr Virgilius.

By this time my conversations with Bernie and Seamus had increased in frequency, with contact virtually on a daily basis. They had spoken to their solicitor and the advice was that if I could put in writing the assurances I had offered in their home, they would co-operate with the production of the programme on Fr Smyth. After consultation with my editor, I was happy to write to them with a detailed break-down of the methods we would use to disguise them from public recognition without sacrificing editorial control. We were able to give the promise that once the edited material had been cut into programme form they could have a private viewing prior to transmission. My visits to their home continued, and eventually I was introduced to their daughter Susan.

In a private conversation about Fr Smyth and my progress with the investigation, Susan mentioned Sarah as someone I should get in touch with regarding St Dominic's School. I told her that I had already spoken to Sarah and it was at this point that Susan hit me with a real stunner: she too had been called out of class at St Dominic's for private meetings with Fr Smyth in a room next to the principal's office, in 1983, 1984 and possibly 1985 – well over a decade after the complaint had been made by Sarah and her parents! This I found utterly astonishing.

Evidence began to emerge of abuses spanning three decades in Belfast. Yet although there had been a promise of action in 1971, here was another individual abused by Fr Smyth stating quite matter-of-factly that over ten years later he was still permitted to enter the school and request of the nuns that girls be brought to him in what had been described as the drawing-room by Sarah. According to Susan the principal at the school during the early part of the eighties was Sr Joan. I had to find this woman.

At this stage I still had not yet made a formal approach to the Catholic Church through their press office in Dublin and so I needed the assistance of individuals with access to various elements in the Church to help me out. In this respect I had one champion, Bernie, and it was Bernie who made the first breakthrough on Sr Joan. She phoned me to say she had been told Sr Joan had left the order to get married and was living somewhere near Cork or Galway. 'Find out more,' I said. 'I have to find this nun!' Bernie undertook to go back to the source for a more precise location and although it took many weeks, she found out exactly where Sr Joan was living: in Galway. She also found out that the earlier information she had received – that Sr Joan had left the order and married – was incorrect.

It was Sunday, 18 September 1994 when I drove into the grounds of the Dominican College, Taylor's Hill, Galway. There were no helpful signs to indicate what was what and there was a choice of three or four doors to knock at. I tried what I thought looked like the living-quarters for the nuns but there was no reply. I drove around the back but there was no sign of life among the old, maybe even disused outsheds and stables. As I drove back around the front, there were cars arriving at the school hall. Inside, a group of girls appeared to be about to begin a play rehearsal. I spoke to a woman I took to be a teacher who directed me back to the door I had first tried. This time there was a stirring inside and the door eventually creaked open; an elderly nun was staring out at me trying to shelter from the rain which was now falling steadily. I asked to speak to Sr Joan and was politely told to come inside to the waiting-room on the right.

Sr Joan, now principal of this school, was much younger than I had expected. She showed no hint of surprise when I explained my business. She said she could recall the incident with Sarah all those years ago at a time when she was a teacher at the Falls Road school. She told me she had been there in all for fifteen years and had experienced some difficult times. She said she was vice-principal from 1977 to 1979 when she succeeded Sr Virgilius as principal, a position she held until 1984 when she moved to Galway. Her version of the story was very different from that given by Sarah and Susan.

In Sr Joan's account, Fr Smyth turned up at the school and asked to see Sarah but as he was seated in the waiting area outside the principal's office, the parlour as she described it, she herself had approached him to ascertain his business. As Sr Joan explained, there was good reason to be conscious of exactly who was coming in and out of the school. Indeed the school had turned parents away on occasion as it was in the interest of the girls not to disturb lessons and not to allow anyone to make unann-ounced arrivals to see pupils. In this instance Sr Joan said the priest mentioned he was a family friend and had promised the girl's family he would call by from time to time. Sarah was sent for but – and this is where Sr Joan's story begins to differ radically from that of Sarah – before going into the room with the priest Sarah told Sr Joan she did not want to see him because 'he did things to her'.

Sr Joan says she accepted the word of the child and stated that she was not going to force a pupil to do something she did not want to do. I asked Sr Joan if she had inquired of Sarah what things was she referring to but she said she had not asked the girl. Accepting the priest's claim that he was a family friend, Sr Joan took the view the problem was because of something going on at home, it certainly did not happen on school premises, and therefore it was a problem to be resolved by the parents. In any event, she mentioned the difficulty to the school principal, Sr Virgilius, who in turn called the girl's family. Sr Joan said there would have been a series of calls but that she was not present for all of them. I asked if she heard Sr Virgilius give any assurance to Sarah's family that the matter would be dealt with by the school and that it would be referred up to a higher Church authority but her reply was that as far as she understood the situation, the family was going to deal with the problem. I went back to Sarah and her family who were livid with anger at the suggestion that the matter had been left in their hands. They had, after all, threatened to go to the police and make public the facts about Fr Smyth's sexual interference with their daughter. They stood firmly by their version of events.

What about Susan's story? Sr Joan was very dismissive of this allegation: in her view it just could not have happened because, in her own words, 'He [Fr Smyth] was never in my school again after that first day,' – in 1971 when Sarah complained. When pressed on Susan's evidence to the police, she did back down a little: 'Of course I cannot possibly account for every moment of every day but to my certain knowledge he was not in the school again.' She offered the view that perhaps the problems with Susan had occurred during a retreat held by Fr Smyth at another school in Belfast, St Rose's. I knew she had already been confronted over the telephone by Susan's mother, Bernie, but nevertheless, my conversation with Sr Joan was continuing to cause me difficulties about exactly what had happened all those years ago.

When I went back to Susan, she was adamant that Fr Smyth had called for her at the school. She went into some detail about one particular incident where he had collected two other girls from St Rose's one day before calling at St Dominic's for her. Susan was called to a room where Fr

Smyth had sexually assaulted her on one occasion. On this particular day, he took her out to his car where she met the other two girls. He took the three girls to Bangor for a meal and after they had eaten he presented each of them with a silver cross with three different coloured stones. Susan says her favourite colour at the time was blue and one of her two companions had been given the cross with the blue stone and in spite of her pleas could not be persuaded to swap. I asked Susan how she could be so precise in her memory. 'Because,' she told me, 'it was my eleventh birthday, 5 June 1983.' So, like Sarah and her family, Susan stands firm behind her version of events at St Dominic's.

As Sr Joan discussed the story I had been given by Susan, she dropped a bombshell. Explaining that she knew nothing further about Fr Smyth until the story broke about his difficulties with the police in Northern Ireland, Sr Joan casually let it be known she had spoken during the summer with Sr Virgilius! In fact she and Sr Virgilius had spoken around the time the Church solicitors were seeking statements of facts from them about their knowledge of Fr Brendan Smyth. I explained the reason for my astonishment: was Sr Virgilius not deceased some time ago? I was assured she was very much alive and working still within the Dominican Order. The earlier information, it now emerged, was inaccurate. Could I speak to her? Where could I find her? That, I was told would not be possible right now as Sr Virgilius had moved to Africa during the summer. Was there not a telephone number where she could be reached? No, that was not possible, even though Sr Joan understood the importance of my reason for wishing to speak to her. When I asked Sr Joan if she would record an interview stating what she had just told me, she said she would get in touch once she had referred to her authorities for guidance. I am still awaiting her reply.

I was uneasy as I left Galway. Could Sarah and Susan have been mistaken? I was reassured when I spoke to them, but in order to make absolutely certain of my facts, I made another check. If these young women had repeated these allegations to the police, they in turn would have confronted Fr Smyth. My checks revealed that one of the charges against him related to one instance of abuse inside St Dominic's; another allegation had been put to him but was not proceeded with in court. In any event, he admitted both, and in relation to Sarah's accusation he told detectives the means by which he could get nuns to deliver, albeit innocently, a girl to a room for him. He said: 'As a priest, I would be known in the sense . . . cause, may have given, well, I would have been known in the sense I would not necessarily have to be known to this individual, you know, nun or that one.' A rambling, incoherent answer perhaps . . . but much of the conversation during the interview was of this nature.

He did recall going to St Dominic's, seeing a nun and requesting an opportunity to speak to Sarah alone. When asked where that meeting would have taken place, he responded: 'Some office or some room down by the office, or something like that.' A policeman asked if it would have been a drawing-room (Sarah's description), and Fr Smyth replied: 'It was a regular sitting-room all right of some sort.' When questioned about Sally's allegation that he had been given access to a room at the Cross and Passion School, he admitted he had use of such a room but he told police he did not accept her assertion that he had locked the door. It is worth pointing out that while I was preparing a programme about Fr Smyth before he had come to trial, I had in fact from an early stage quietly established from sources that the priest had from the outset admitted the charges against him. I did not have any moral or ethical dilemmas as I continued researching the life and times of Fr Brendan Smyth.

After just a few weeks, I had built up a profile of the paedophile priest, and in conversation with those he had abused or with members of their families, I acquired more and more information worth checking up. He had been in Rome in the late 1940s or early 1950s and there had been rumours of complaints there as well. There were whispers in the side streets of West Belfast of other families experiencing difficulties and questions about how he had so much freedom to travel to Belfast from County Cavan, to pick up children and go away for weekends but there was much still unknown about him. One of the most intriguing questions concerned his travels to the United States. There was nothing he enjoyed more than to regale his friends and acquaintances with tales of his adventures in America. Bernie knew someone who had received a Christmas card from the priest whilst he was on pastoral duties in the United States. The card came from Langdon, North Dakota. My challenge was to find out more about his work there without alerting the Catholic authorities as I was not yet fully prepared to put questions to those who had control over the priest. I was about to make another series of startling discoveries when I began my inquiries on the other side of the Atlantic.

5

PORN IN THE USA

When the information came to us from you in Ireland regarding Fr Smyth and allegations of sexual misconduct there and the pending trial, I contacted our Vicar General, Fr Wendelin Vetter, immediately and we re-opened the investigation into these matters that came to us a year ago. Fr Vetter faxed me a letter to be read to the congregation informing the congregation of Fr Smyth's allegations and pending trial in Ireland and inviting any of our members since he had served in this parish to come forward with any experiences or concerns they might have had about suffering sexual abuse either themselves or their children, so that proper counselling and help could be provided for them.

Fr Dale Kinzler, St Alphonsus Church, Langdon, North Dakota, describing his response to my queries about Fr Smyth on Monday, 28 February 1994. (The Vicar General's letter was read out in Church on 5 March.)

Bob Simmons owns a radio station in Langdon, North Dakota. I came to meet him because of my desire to track down the parish where Fr Brendan Smyth had served, in a manner which would not arouse any interest in the Church itself. I reasoned that if I made my initial approach through official channels, it would start alarm bells ringing before I was ready to set them off. I wanted to establish for myself facts concerning the activities of Fr Smyth, to prepare my own profile, my own dossier. As it turned out, my attempt to proceed in this direction was unnecessary as the Church in the United States was more than willing to answer questions openly about such problems, at least more openly than the Church in Ireland had been over the years.

My first call was to the offices of ITN in Washington to discover if anyone there could help me get in touch with a journalist, a discreet individual, in North Dakota and the closer he or she might be situated to Langdon, the better. Looking after the ITN office was a young man called Andy Brattle who promised help but asked for time to make some check calls. In truth, I didn't expect to hear from him for a few days but he was back on the line within a few hours ... and with a result. He had checked around and found there was a newspaper in a place called Cavalier, thirty minutes from Langdon by car, and there was a radio station in Langdon itself. I was soon to encounter the hard news edge of Bob Simmons, proprietor of KYND-1080, the affiliate station of ABC.

With trepidation I dialled the telephone number supplied by Andy. I was initially put through to news editor Bruce Allen who listened with interest to my story, although I was not prepared to give too much away at this early stage. I simply wanted to know if a Fr Brendan Smyth had served in the local Catholic parish in the period 1980 to 1983. I explained he was facing allegations in Ireland and I was quietly attempting to find out if there had been any hint of a similar problem during his tour of duty, if indeed there had been a tour of duty.

Bruce soon switched me over to his boss and quick as a flash Bob Simmons was telling me there was a hint that something was amiss around the departure of the Irish priest. He could not put his finger on anything but offered to make a few calls to refresh his memory.

In the meantime he was keen to know more about the problem in Ireland. It was crunch time for me: was I to trust this man with more information about the priest, or should I hold back. I decided I had to take a chance, explaining to Bob that what we were about to discuss was for our ears only and that if any of the allegations in Belfast were to be proven in court I, in exchange for some assistance now, would be prepared to provide him with full details from my side of the Atlantic. I would even do a voice report from Belfast. He agreed to this plan, but suddenly I was aware of electronic clicking noises on the line midway through the next section of the conversation: Bob was taping our chat. I threatened to hang up in protest but he insisted this was a matter of form at the station's newsdesk and that the material would never be used for broadcast. Another thing that troubled me was that even though Bob had a recollection of a problem with the priest in the past, he could not offer any reasonable explanation for this conviction and he seemed to be stalling when asked to provide names. I had told him I wanted any inquiries made on my behalf to be done in a discreet manner and suggested that at this stage it might be as well not to go directly to the local church. We concluded in this way: Bob was going to make some calls and come back to me later that night; I provided my home number.

He was as good as his word and I had hardly got myself settled in front of my notebooks and the television set when the telephone rang. Yes, says Bob, there were suspicions of a problem but he could not be any more precise. When I asked whom he had been speaking to he declined to say but when I ventured a guess that he had been in touch with the local priest his negative answer was far from being convincing. Further suspicion grew in my mind about his comment that this was a good news story for his station and I was not at all prepared to believe his weak attempt to tell me that he would wait until we reached a stage where we could mutually agree to publication. Worse still, when I said I would like to speak to his informant, said I would have to do that if we were to run the story, he became very coy. When I replaced the receiver, I resolved to make my own inquiries.

Once I had found out the diocese where the parish of Langdon was situated it did not take long before I was chatting to a very kind lady in the diocesan headquarters who provided me with invaluable assistance to get me to the parish priest at St Alphonsus. She told me the man I wanted to talk to was Fr Dale Kinzler. It was the last day of February, 1994. I decided to assist my ailing shorthand by taping my call to Fr Kinzler. It was not a very good quality recording, but my memory and my notebook served me well. I was amazed at the openness of Fr Kinzler, who in a matter-of-fact manner informed me that there had been problems with Fr Smyth, problems which had surfaced in the parish a year earlier. Investigation had not been advanced by the Church even though he reported the allegations on house calls to Fr Wendelin Vetter, the Vicar General and the man appointed by the Bishop of Fargo, Dr James Sullivan, to supervise investigations of any sex abuse allegations.

Initially, there had been three families with concerns about Fr Smyth, families who had befriended the Irish priest known to possess an enthusiasm for traditional Church values, someone who had set about restoring rosary beads to their proper place within the congregation of St Alphonsus and who had become involved in the spiritual care of the young through his work with the altar boys. Fr Kinzler spoke bluntly and, as I was to learn, factually, about the problem his parish had faced. He identified the boys at risk as those in the fourth to eighth school grades, in other words boys in the ten to fourteen age-group. He was able to recall that the previous bishop, Dr Driscoll, by then deceased, may have learned of complaints about the priest although as yet nothing had shown up on the records. Nevertheless Fr Kinzler was able to give me the number of a priest who had served in the parish around the same time as Fr Smyth and who had apparently stated that the Irish priest had been removed from the parish under a cloud. No one seemed to know exactly what circumstances pertained at the time of his return to Ireland in 1983. It may be hard to explain but I had this buzz of excitement, not because the priest had allegedly abused children in the United States, but because we had tracked him down to a foreign land in the early 1980s where he was permitted to go by his Church authorities after he had been revealed as a molester at St Dominic's in 1971.

Fr Kinzler explained the circumstances in which he became aware of the allegations. It appears that after a neighbouring diocese faced a million-dollar lawsuit over sex-abuse allegations, the Fargo diocese wanted to ensure there were no problems waiting to sneak up on them in the years ahead. They decided to confront the issue and parish priests were instructed to engage in a programme of door-to-door calls. The programme was entitled *Open Hearts, Open Minds* and during his house calls, Fr Kinzler heard from three families with quite definite problems relating to the Irish priest. Three others said they had become aware of risks with the priest and had taken their own preventive action, withdrawing their children from the altar boy programme. Fr Kinzler was not in Langdon during Fr Smyth's time but he said he met Fr Smyth 'four or five years ago when he was here on vacation.'

Following my chat with Fr Kinzler I decided to contact Fr Vetter to see how the official investigation was proceeding. I did not make contact with him until Wednesday, 2 March 1994 and it was a worrying experience. He began by stating he did not understand my interest, because as far as he was aware there were no formal complaints on file against Fr Smyth. He confessed to having known the priest as a personal friend, someone he had visited in Ireland at one stage, and a man he referred to as 'Fr Gerry'.

'Fr Gerry' was not a diocesan priest; he was on loan

from Kilnacrott Abbey but did perform pastoral duties whilst in North Dakota. According to Fr Vetter the agreements for such arrangements rest between the bishop of the diocese and the religious superior of the order concerned, in this case Abbot Kevin Smith (no relation of Fr Smyth) of Kilnacrott Abbey in County Cavan who enjoyed a rank equivalent to a bishop. When I asked if the Catholic Church as one of the biggest employers in the world had any method of passing on the personnel records of its staff, he said that would be done between the exchanging bishops so they alone would be aware of the precise details of the individuals concerned, although once in place the diocese would open a file on the person they had borrowed. It was interesting that Fr Vetter believed Fr Smyth had seen service in the parish at an earlier time, possibly as early as 1976, although again there was no record to confirm this view.

This conversation with Fr Vetter was not exactly encouraging – for two reasons. Firstly, the denial of any complaints flew in the face of the story from Fr Kinzler who seemed open and sure that there had been problems with the Irish priest. This denial put me on edge: why this blatant contradiction? I had to resolve this quandary one way or another.

Thursday, 3 March 1994, was an uneasy day; because of the time difference between here and that part of the United States (they are five hours behind us), I had to wait until after midnight to make contact for a second time with Fr Kinzler of North Dakota. I had decided that as a matter of tactics I would not at first mention my call to Fr Vetter so that Fr Kinzler would be free to state once again the facts as he knew them. Of course, had he made any effort to backtrack on what he had previously told me, I should have known he had either exaggerated the stories or that he had been told by higher authorities to keep quiet.

Fr Kinzler did not retract one word and as the conversation continued he actually provided additional information as I gently probed for more detail about the specifics of the complaints. He explained that the first complaint had come from the aunt of a young man who had been abused when twelve years of age. The aunt told Fr Kinzler that she was reluctant to have him contact the family so Fr Kinzler says he told her to talk to her brother (the young man's father) and encourage them to take the matter further by approaching the diocese of Fargo directly. According to Fr Kinzler the family found a way of getting in touch with Fr Smyth in Ireland. He told me he would later go into further detail about this case. I tried to get him to give details of the result of the contacts with Fr Smyth but he said I should have to wait until later.

The second complaint made to him concerned a mother becoming suspicious about her son's sudden reluctance to continue his work with Fr Smyth as an altar boy at the church. This made her observe more closely the pattern of the training meetings organised by Fr Smyth. They had become more frequent and were getting longer and longer, and for this reason she started to go to them herself to keep an eye on things. The boy was removed from the altar servers scheme after he began having nightmares, waking up mumbling. His mother asked her other son, who slept in the same room, to listen to what he was saying when he was wakened by his nightmares. It turned out that the boy was saying, 'No, Fr Smyth, no!' Fr Kinzler pointed out that on being questioned the boy did not make any allegation of sexual abuse.

The third complaint was from a mother who became very alarmed by Fr Smyth's habit of reaching his hands into the trousers of her son and apparently fondling his bottom. Fr Kinzler said he had received numerous reports of this type of behaviour but it was this one mother who became sufficiently concerned to make contact with someone she trusted. She went to the former pastor, the man who had preceded Fr Smyth at St Alphonsus in Langdon. It was this complaint, according to Fr Kinzler, which was passed on to Bishop Justin Driscoll by the pastor and which subsequently led to Fr Smyth's removal from his pastorate. Fr Kinzler even went as far as to say that given the year this report was made to the bishop, 1983, neither the bishop nor Church officials, would have known what management steps to take to ensure there would be no further abuse in the diocese. He said the present bishop (Dr Sullivan) took sex-abuse allegations very seriously and had introduced a programme for the removal of any priests accused of misconduct of this kind.

When I asked him if he felt disappointed or in some way let down by the Church authorities in Ireland who had responsibility for permitting Fr Smyth to travel to North Dakota without first warning the Church in America of his propensity to abuse children sexually, Fr Kinzler said: 'It's very painful and unfortunate to know that those who suffered abuse here might have been free of it if Bishop Driscoll had known, and in turn if the proper information had been conveyed from us to Ireland upon his return that further abuses might also have been prevented. So there would have been at best a communication gap, at worst some kind of irresponsible management of that procedure of release of the pastor.' Damning words indeed, and although I had not yet met Fr Kinzler face to face, the overwhelming impression over the telephone was that of a man at peace with the world, a world where he valued the truth above all else, a priest who seemed free to speak his mind and to recognise the value of truth.

When I eventually told him of my concerns after my chat with Fr Vetter, he said this was possibly the position at the moment because after the initial complaints, no one was prepared to go forward to the bishop or to Fr Vetter, but there had been complaints and Fr Kinzler reckoned there would be individuals prepared to talk to me. I was reassured and consoled by the willingness of Fr Kinzler to find out if anyone would speak to me but he could make no promises. Fr Kinzler said all clerics in the diocese from the bishop down wanted to ensure justice was done. Indeed, as a result of my first telephone call to him on the Monday (28 February 1994), Fr Vetter had ordered a letter to be read out in church the following Sunday, 5 March. This is what Fr Vetter wanted congregations in the Fargo diocese to hear:

Dear Parishioners of St Alphonsus, Langdon and St Edwards, Nekoma

Your parishes were among those served by Fr John Smyth while he was in the Diocese of Fargo. The diocese became aware just recently that Fr

Smyth has been charged in Belfast, Ireland with sexual misconduct with a young boy. We are not aware of the full particulars of the charge. We understand there possibly will be a criminal trial in mid-March in Belfast.

We are truly concerned that similar misconduct may have occurred while Father was serving in your parishes. If you have any knowledge of such conduct, or if you have been the victim of such conduct, please contact us immediately. If you wish, we will treat your report confidentially. The diocese is willing to help anyone who may have been hurt. We urge you to contact any of the following:- your Pastor, Fr Kinzler; Sr Ann O'Brien, telephone 701-235-7279, or myself, Fr Vetter, 701-237-6063. You need not identify yourself, until you are ready to do so.

We are sorry for any hurt and injury that may have been caused. In no way does the diocese condone actions such as this. Do know that our prayers will be with you all during this difficult time.

Here is the evidence of how the American Catholic Church in North Dakota was prepared to deal with the problem of paedophilia. In fact, Fr Kinzler said two new cases against Smyth emerged after this letter was read and one of them was, he said, a 'very serious case of sexual assault against a girl'. Perhaps there is a lesson to be learned from this willingness to confront the issue head-on.

During the next few weeks I made several calls to North Dakota, speaking not only to Fr Kinzler and Fr Vetter, but also to Bishop Sullivan, who explained how Fr Smyth's temporary transfer to North Dakota would have been arranged. He said that priests coming in to do pastoral work would have all their details passed on by the 'provincial' or leader of the religious order to which he belonged, in this case Abbot Kevin Smith, to the bishop where the priest was being sent. 'Normally only those considered good risks are sent,' he said.

By 21 March Fr Kinzler was able to report that one key family where a teenage altar boy had been abused by Fr Smyth would perhaps be willing to speak to me about their experience of the priest. They had been forced to leave Langdon to try to rebuild their lives. With the promise of interviews 'on camera' from Fr Kinzler, Fr Vetter and even the bishop, Dr James Sullivan, I knew a trip to the United States would be worthwhile. As yet there was no guarantee of an interview from any of those alleging abuse against Fr Smyth; indeed, I had not at this stage even spoken to any of them on the telephone, but given the sensitive nature of the investigation, I firmly believed I should take a chance on going out. It would be easier to speak face-to-face to those abused by Fr Smyth and to assure them of our motives for covering the story and of our ability to protect their identities. In this respect, I was given the full support of UTV.

My final calls to America prior to making the journey were on 21 March, when I confirmed arrangements to meet an American camera-crew and to finalise the times and dates for interviews with Fr Kinzler, Fr Vetter and Bishop Sullivan. There was also time to meet members of the congregation at St Alphonsus, some of whom still supported Fr Smyth and who were struggling to reconcile the news from

Ireland with the memories they had of the good works done by the Irish priest. But even before I left these shores, Bob Simmons came back to haunt me, for during one of my calls to Fr Kinzler, I discovered that Bob had broadcast an interview with me! He had actually gone ahead and used a section of the interview he told me was recorded as a matter of routine. I telephoned the radio station to moan about this breach of trust which I thought might still have the potential to severely damage my own inquiries. Bob apologised and I accepted, once I heard the edited clip he had put on air. It was difficult to fall out with Bob and I was still looking forward very much to meeting him ... but I would be circumspect in what I told him in future.

The trip to North Dakota was planned for Palm Sunday weekend beginning on 25 March. I still had not learned the secret Fr Kinzler was holding back about the Langdon family who had confronted Fr Smyth directly by letter – that surprise still lay ahead.

6
≡

LANGDON CITY LIMITS

*Even before we heard about Fr Smyth from you we
did update our procedures considerably. In fact, we
were one of the first dioceses in the country to have
seminars for our priests, bring in psychologists and
lawyers to talk to them about this problem that was
developing and at the same time we put together in
1987 or '88 one of the first sets of guidelines to be
followed in the case of any accusations of sex abuse
or exploitation.*

*Bishop James Sullivan, North Dakota, USA (during an
interview with the author on Monday 28 March 1994)*

Hanging around Minneapolis Airport for four hours
waiting for a connecting flight to Grand Forks is not a fun
thing to do. The airport was designed by someone who
clearly did not envisage travellers having to spend more
than a penny in the place.

Grand Forks airport is about the same size as the city
airport in Belfast. You know the type of place: one book-

shop which in this case doubles as the café. When I got there about ten at night it was snowing and bitterly cold. My intention was to pick up a hire car at the airport and drive a short distance to an hotel on the outskirts of the city to rest before tackling the remainder of the journey to Langdon, still about 120 miles away.

Highway 29 runs right alongside the Ramada Inn and the northbound carriageway leads ultimately to Winnipeg in Canada 150 miles away, but a left turn about two-thirds of the way towards the Canadian border takes you on to Highway 5 near the town of Hamilton, through Cavalier and finally to Langdon. I slipped a tape into the cassette player on the dashboard and listened to recordings of the Fr Vetter telephone interviews as I sped towards Langdon and Fr Brendan Smyth's secret American past.

Entering Langdon you are welcomed to a 'city' of 2,500 souls and as you pass the 'city limits' sign by a large filling station you notice immediately the church spire which dominates the skyline. This is St Alphonsus Church, a useful landmark.

Home for the priests of St Alphonsus is the rectory next door to the church and as I reached the front door a parishioner was leaving bidding 'Fr Dale' goodbye. I offered out my hand, he said something like, 'You must be Chris,' as he guided me inside. Fr Dale Kinzler looked like a man in his late twenties or early thirties with a shock of wiry black hair. Getting straight to the point, he informed me of his recent interviews for the local television station in Grand Forks who had somehow picked up on the Fr Smyth story and, leading me into the lounge, he played a video recording of the news bulletin.

Fr Kinzler chatted about his progress in finding one of those abused by Fr Smyth prepared to do an interview and the sad reality was, as things stood at this moment, that no one had given a firm undertaking even to speak to me. He said he would continue to make representations on my behalf. As he had been in all previous conversations on this subject, Fr Kinzler was extremely cautious about letting the name of any individual slip from his tongue.

The Channel 8 news coverage was interesting but no threat to our story; so it was with a feeling of relief that we had not been scooped that I was shown round the church by Fr Kinzler and listened as he explained that there would be two Masses next morning, Palm Sunday. Arrangements had been made to meet a television crew from Grand Forks at the Langdon Motor Inn at around eight o'clock so we could get our equipment organised inside the church before the worshippers arrived. As we set out the ground rules for movement of the crew during the services, Fr Kinzler revealed that some members of the congregation who had been particularly close to Fr Smyth had difficulty believing what they had been hearing of the priest's problems back in Ireland and I made a mental note to seek out some of those who could not believe the horrific news from Ireland.

It might have been twenty below in a blizzard outside but inside St Alphonsus the warmth of the welcome was matched by the colour of the Palm Sunday services which opened with Fr Kinzler leading children carrying palm leaves down the main aisle of the church.

Organist Cindy Johnston did not have to work so hard on this day as musical interludes were provided by a group of enthusiastic gospel singers using guitars and a tambourine. Cindy and her husband Terry had special reasons for having fond memories of Fr Smyth: the priest had catechised Terry in preparation for his entry into the Catholic faith and when Cindy was giving birth to their first child Fr Smyth spent most of the twenty-one hours of a very difficult labour with Cindy, encouraging her through prayer to believe there would be no complications or difficulties. As a result, they had given their first-born son an Irish name, Arran.

Cindy was visibly nervous as the camera crew hovered behind her, recording her playing during the first Mass at 9.30 am. The second Mass was due to get under way an hour later and we used the time in between to interview a few people who had only good memories of the work done by Fr Smyth, people like Thomas Mann who praised the Irish priest for restoring many of the traditional Catholic forms at St Alphonsus Church. He said it was difficult to accept that the man who was his friend all those years ago and who had played a major part in bringing rosary beads into vogue again had done all the things he had been accused of doing. Like many others, Mr Mann spoke of his fatherly image and held that it would be very natural to see him with children, touching them in many ways in the playground, the kind of contact associated with a caring and kind person. This faith in Fr Smyth was commendable in a friend but even when it was pointed out that there had been some similar problems in Langdon and that Fr Smyth had made admissions to police back in Ireland, Mr Mann stoutly defended his old friend as someone who took time to work tirelessly on behalf of the parishioners of St Alphonsus. On the question of the local allegations, he said it was always difficult to deal with children who were capable at times of exacting revenge on adults who for some reason, often unknown, had offended against the child. He said he would reserve his judgement until after Fr Smyth's trial.

Kathleen and Bill Delvo were among the closest of Fr Smyth's friends during his pastoral posting to Langdon and when the priest left for Ireland in 1983, they stored his belongings until he was ready to have them sent on to County Cavan. As others quietly prayed at the front of the church during the break between services, we chatted with this kindly couple at the back of the church. At one stage during the interview, Kathleen was almost moved to tears as she tried to express the thought that at this time the people of Langdon must pray for those children locally who had been abused by Fr Smyth but should also spare a thought and a prayer for the priest. This couple displayed great dignity in the manner in which they had come to terms with the grief caused by a paedophile and even though they found it hard to believe he had been abusing children while visiting their home regularly as a close and trusted friend, they seemed resigned to the harsh reality of truth and yes, they did feel a sense of betrayal.

Once the last worshippers left the church to rush home through the freezing snowfall outside to Sunday lunch, it was time to set up our interview with Fr Kinzler. Even though I had spent many hours on the telephone getting his side of the story, I was not prepared for everything he had to say. He explained that Fr Smyth's charges in

Ireland had resulted in feelings of both disappointment and relief among his parishioners. Disappointment in the sense of discovering something they did not know about a priest who was admired by many members of the St Alphonsus congregation for his great rapport with the more traditional Catholics identifying with Fr Smyth's personal spiritual style. Relief in the sense that others who had long been silently suffering from the priest's abuses were now being offered the opportunity to seek justice and help to establish what Fr Kinzler described as 'some kind of healing process through the offer of counselling from the diocese'. Even as we spoke, he said, there was an ongoing search for anyone who had been involved in the altar servers' programme as it appears that it was through this that Fr Smyth singled out his victims.

In the case of the most serious sexual misconduct, Fr Kinzler explained he had experienced most pain because this family had felt betrayed and alienated by the Church, making a conscious decision to quit attending Mass and frightened to approach any priest for fear the contact might result in a repetition of what had happened in the past. At this point I asked Fr Kinzler if any of those abused by Fr Smyth had been able to have any kind of confrontation with the priest. His answer astounded me. This is what he had been hinting at on the telephone days before I set off for the United States. His answer is given below in full:

The one that did have confrontation with Fr Smyth, that is the first one that came to my attention, obtained his address through other friends that had gotten Christmas cards from him. The father wrote to Fr Smyth noting that his son was receiving counselling and that there was considerable financial investment in that counselling and Fr Smyth did respond with a gift, a relatively small gift of $500 (five hundred dollars). So in asking for further assistance with that counselling, Fr Smyth responded with four gifts of five thousand dollars each over the period of the next two years and that gift series has recently terminated in light of the situation now.

The implications of this statement left me momentarily stunned. Fr Smyth had paid a total of $20,000 (twenty thousand dollars) to a young man he had abused as an altar boy in St Alphonsus many years earlier. My mind raced: where did a priest who had taken a vow of poverty find this money?

What reason had he given the family for ending the flow of cash? According to Fr Kinzler they were simply told that his circumstances had changed and that he had been forced into retirement. Fr Kinzler wrongly believed that with Fr Smyth admitting such serious charges he would face mandatory expulsion from the Norbertine Order, hence the end of the money supply. The truth is that there is no such rule apparently within the Norbertine Order at Kilnacrott Abbey as Fr Smyth is still regarded as one of their members and is listed as such in the 1995 *Irish Catholic Directory.* Certainly the list of questions I was preparing to put to the Catholic Church authorities in Ireland was growing daily and the time was fast approaching when I would begin the process of putting these questions to the people who had control of Fr Brendan Smyth during his religious life in the Norbertine community. At this stage I still thought that the activities of a religious order within the Catholic Church in Ireland could be made accountable to the Church and its spiritual leader, the Cardinal. It would be some time before I would begin to understand the complexities of the workings of the Church.

However, there was still much to be done in the United States. After being interviewed Fr Kinzler left us to continue filming in the empty church while he went off to keep an appointment and to make yet another inquiry of the family paid the twenty thousand dollars by Fr Smyth. Naturally Fr Kinzler did not want to betray their trust so he could only put me in touch with them if they agreed but it was now a vitally important ingredient in our report since we needed confirmation of the payments and the circumstances of the problems experienced. Before he left, I emphasised to Fr Kinzler just how crucial it now was to have access to the family and I implored him to do his best to persuade them to at least meet me as I believed my powers of persuasion would eventually succeed in bringing about an interview. In the meantime I was preparing myself for my first face-to-face encounter with Bob Simmons. I called him at home and arranged to see him in a local bar at six o'clock and although I instinctively recognised him when he entered, he and his colleague walked past me. I enjoyed the moment as I called them back and we began the process of getting to know each other properly.

We spent the evening together at a local restaurant, Fr Kinzler joining us in time for the main course. Next morning I set off in convoy with the crew for a 300-mile round trip from Langdon to St Anthony's Church in Fargo, where Bishop James Sullivan and Fr Vetter were waiting in the latter's office to be interviewed. The fact they had agreed to face the camera is another clear example of the willingness of the Catholic Church in the United States to face up to the unpalatable reality of problem priests and confront the issue head-on by making themselves publicly accountable for their actions.

St Anthony's was situated in a quiet suburban area. Fr Vetter had someone with him but his secretary showed us into the conference room where the interview was to be recorded and by the time he arrived we were ready to shoot, although there was a further delay whilst we waited for Bishop Sullivan to arrive. As we waited Fr Vetter went to some lengths to explain that he was not in his present post when Fr Smyth first came to North Dakota and he spoke of his surprise that anything like Fr Smyth's sexual misconduct could happen; there was no indication during his time in the United States that anything was amiss.

The bishop arrived and the interview got under way with an explanation from Fr Vetter about why Fr Smyth had been sent from Ireland. The previous bishop, Dr Justin Driscoll, identified a shortage of priests and had been in contact with the Norbertine Order in Ireland, or to be exact, with Abbot Kevin Smith, the religious superior of the community at Kilnacrott Abbey. According to Fr Vetter, they initially wanted to send over a number of priests to be placed in parishes side by side, where they could visit each other and create a small community of their own. Fr Smyth was the first to come over in 1979 but it took at least another three years to get another priest, Fr Paul Madden, over from Kilnacrott. As Fr Vetter said the idea for a community of Irish priests did not work out and the plans were scrapped.

Both men were clearly stung by the unwelcome publicity attached to Fr Smyth's period of pastoral service in Langdon and were clear that at no time was the Church in America made aware of Fr Smyth's history as a paedophile before, during or after his stay. I admit to having had difficulty believing this, and pressed them hard to explain to me how one of the world's largest employers could move staff all around the globe without having in place some kind of personnel system which would indicate to everyone concerned with the supply of priests the individual's record of employment. To be frank, it was almost inconceivable there was no mention of Fr Smyth's record as a child molester when Abbot Smith sent him out here to North Dakota but the Americans were adamant that nothing had shown up on the file to suggest any problem and they were uncertain if the late Bishop Driscoll ever sent any message back to Ireland that their priest had been misbehaving. I asked the bishop if there was any system of personnel management and he said: 'Personnel management in the sense that the bishop [Driscoll] would contact the head of the religious order [Abbot Kevin Smith] and ask if there is anything wrong, if they knew of anything which would mean they could not recommend the priest. So far as we knew everything was fine. He belonged to the Norbertines and our bishop asked the Abbot or the Abbot General who was recommending him, and that is how it worked.' Anything formally in writing? 'Not that I know of,' said Bishop Sullivan. 'I didn't find anything at all in the records here. All I discovered was the employment record of Fr Smyth, that he had been working in a retreat house in Dublin – that sort of thing – but there was nothing to indicate any problems.'

The bishop was at pains to emphasise that his diocese was among the first in the United States to establish seminars for priests, to get expert opinion on the whole issue of paedophilia from lawyers and psychologists in the latter half of the eighties, prompted to do so by the activities of an attorney in the neighbouring diocese of Minneapolis-St Paul, who was prepared actively to pursue the Church through the courts for a settlement of a case involving a man called Anderson. As Bishop Sullivan explained: 'Up to that time paedophilia was something that wasn't even in the vocabulary of our people. In fact, I know a counsellor who did not even know what the word meant – she had to look it up – so it is something that is very recent as far as the Church history is concerned. We wanted to educate our priests to be aware this was happening and to let them consider their own habits of relating to other people: how they had to act so there would be concern and awareness and obviously we did not want anyone to be hurt in the process.' He said the bishops in America had met at least four times to discuss this new problem confronting the Church throughout the country and it had put them on guard when recruiting for the priesthood. Vetting had been intensified to try to weed out those who might be tempted to apply because of their sexual preferences for children.

In the course of the interview Fr Vetter said he had just recently met the family who had been paid twenty thousand dollars by Fr Smyth. This in his view was a clear indication of Fr Smyth's guilt although he went on to say that once he met the young man there was no room for doubt about that guilt. Mention of this particular case reminded me that as yet I had not heard from the family and my return journey was booked for next day, the Tuesday. But what I did not realise as I bade farewell to the two clergymen in Fargo was that the father of the abused boy had been trying to contact me by telephone back in the hotel at Langdon and in making the long journey back north I actually drove through Grand Forks, where he lived since moving out of Langdon on discovering that his son had been abused. However, I was delighted to hear he had been looking for me and while the crew broke for coffee, I was busy on the telephone. This was my last chance to use my powers of persuasion to secure the one interview which would be the icing on my North Dakota cake.

Bill, the father, told me his son had been sexually abused whilst an altar server at St Alphonsus Church in Langdon and had suffered the pain and humiliation in silence until it overwhelmed him in more recent times when a problem arose in his marriage. At first Bill seemed determined to turn down any requests for an interview but I sensed his feeling of anger and betrayal when I spelled out the extent of Fr Smyth's abuses back in Ireland. I was able to tell him of the evidence that he had abused persistently over a period of three decades and that he had occasion to be sent for treatment. At least that is what had been stated by Cardinal Daly in a letter I had seen from the family who received it in 1992. As yet I did not have a copy of the letter as the family concerned, Bernie and Seamus, did not want to release it publicly, a position they maintained right up to the programme deadline some five or six months later.

In any event, mention of these facts did have a profound effect on Bill, who now was more receptive to the argument that he almost had a duty to speak out and make known publicly his criticism not only of the Church in America but of the Church authorities responsible for Fr Smyth in Ireland. I promised identity protection and offered to drive straight back to Grand Forks if he could be persuaded at least to meet me. His anger that his son had been hurt and humiliated even though the Church authorities back in Ireland knew of Fr Smyth's propensity to sexually abuse children was the decisive factor in his next move. He said he did not want me to drive to his home until he had first spoken to his son and to their lawyer.

I sipped coffee in the hotel reception as the minutes became hours and still no word. Eventually Bill made contact and offered me the telephone numbers of his lawyer in Grand Forks. I knew I was virtually back where I had started with Bill and would now have to go through the whole thing again if I was to make this visit really successful. I had known from the start of this trip to the United States that there was no guarantee of an interview with anyone abused by Fr Smyth and I thought I was mentally prepared for the eventuality that all I would have would be interviews with Fr Kinzler, some parishioners, Bishop Sullivan and Fr Vetter. When I realised that I was going to be heading home without the direct evidence of Fr Smyth's abuses in America I knew I would feel that I had partly failed in my mission.

Bill's lawyer, Lee Hamilton, used his legal skills to probe my motives in wishing to speak to his clients and I spent almost forty-five minutes during that first call trying to reassure him that I could provide protection for his clients, disguise their appearance and their voices. I stressed how important it was to expose the fact that if the Church authorities in Ireland had reacted differently to Fr Smyth's paedophilia his client would have escaped his abuses, I stressed the deadline I faced – I was due to travel home first thing next morning – but if I thought there was a chance to meet his clients I would stay another night providing he could give me sufficient notice. I replaced the receiver for one of the longest two hours in my life. When the call finally came through, Lee said he could guarantee nothing until he had met me personally. If I could provide him with a list of questions and explain how I could protect his clients and if he liked what I had to say he would produce his clients at our hotel near the airport for interview. I was to be at the hotel by eleven next day. It was not a yes but then again it was not a no. I went to bed happy that at least there was still hope.

Lee Hamilton was late for our rendezvous at the Ramada Inn in Grand Forks and by the time he arrived I had consumed six cups of coffee and I was about to have lunch. As my toasted sandwich was set before me he ordered something similar with French fries on the side.

By now I was getting extremely nervous as my flight out of Grand Forks was scheduled to leave in a few hours' time and still I had no agreement for an interview with anyone abused by Fr Smyth.

During lunch the tables turned as I found myself being bombarded with questions from the lawyer about our programme, our intentions and what guarantees we would give his clients. It was touch and go for over an hour as I made my pitch. Finally he agreed to an interview provided I would formally write out the questions and fax them to his office downtown while he met his clients for a short conference. Once the questions were received and they had a short chat about them he would bring his clients to the hotel where we would have already set up our filming equipment in a room so that we did not draw attention to his clients in full sight of the public. Hallelujah! Once Lee left the hotel the crew was despatched to set up for interviews in a ground floor room close to the indoor swimming pool while my flight was rearranged for next day. The questions were written out and faxed to Lee's office.

When Lee returned with his clients a couple of hours later he presented me with a typed sheet of paper setting out the terms of agreement for the interviews. They sought my assurance that they would be disguised and that any tapes sent back to the United States would not include their actual voices. I signed both copies and thought I was now ready to begin but Lee interrupted with a list of questions his clients would not answer: they confirmed that they had received the payment of $20,000 but declined to take questions about the money during the interview.

Dave had only just begun answering my second question when tears started running down his cheeks. He said he had met Fr Smyth when he was an altar boy in 1979, describing the priest as a strict disciplinarian who set tough tests for the boys engaged in the scheme. It was not long before the abuse started, although when I asked Dave what exactly happened he could barely answer as the sobbing increased in intensity. I realised this might just be too painful for lucid recollection. He managed to say: 'Just mainly fondling and just, he would . . . just things. I mean it was mainly fondling.' Here was a grown man sobbing at the thought of his normal, happy childhood being ruined by the actions of a man with no scruples and no concern about the dreadful agony he left behind. Now in his mid-twenties and married with two children of his own, Dave had been too scared to tell anyone, preferring to hold his silence and bear the hurt – that is until 1992 when he could contain this awful secret no longer and confessed to his wife and parents. Dave had rationalised his silent suffering of Fr Smyth's activities because of the terrified confusion they caused in a youngster brought up as a Catholic to believe that priests were above reproach. In a small town where his abuser was clearly so popular and admired, who would ever believe a twelve-year-old child. 'How do you go against the Church?' he asked. 'How do you go against a priest who is supposed to be, as children in the Catholic faith are taught, the next step to God. They are the ones you talk to, then they talk to God. He's supposed to be better than anybody else. You don't think they are human, but they are, that's what people must realise, the people inside the churches are just the same as outside the Church.

'Priests are next to God; you don't think they are human but they are.' Such is the effect of the Church on its young parishioners; this is the way they view men of the cloth. Fr Smyth was able to use that position to gain the trust of twelve-year-olds like Dave, to use his power to ensure children would be all but incapable of blowing his cover. Dave said Fr Smyth was able to transfer his own guilt on to him and for thirteen years he kept the priest's secret. It was time to speak out now to alter that attitude, to make sure the victims get help and the guilty get punished.

Psychologically, Dave has grown to detest the Church; he simply does not trust it and will not allow his children to be raised in the Catholic faith. Undoubtedly his views were formulated during the thirteen years he felt like a lost soul on earth, like the guilty party to a dreadful secret. 'I find it hard to trust people,' he told me, 'especially males. I have only a couple of close male friends; I get on better with females and that's hard for my wife to go through. It almost wrecked our marriage until I came out and that's one of the reasons I came out: to save my marriage and my family.' When Dave said he wanted to see Fr Smyth put in jail for a very long time so 'he can't hurt any more kids,' you realised he was enraged at what had been inflicted on him by the priest. Today, he says he is very protective of his own two children and will not allow strangers to go anywhere near them. He admits that it is an unhealthy attitude which could in some way adversely mark his children for life. Dave insisted on passing on a message to any children back in Ireland who might hear his words on television. This is what he had to tell them: 'Go and talk to someone. Sure, it is scary but it is nothing to be embarrassed about. It is not your fault; it is this person's fault. Just keep telling people until somebody believes you: a teacher, a parent, anybody, a family member or the police, anybody, just talk to them and keep telling people until someone believes you and just be totally honest about it.'

This had been a distressing interview because of Dave's obvious discomfort and pain, and as it finished his father Bill was waiting to give him a hug, as if to emphasise the family support which had been galvanised in the light of Dave's experiences. Bill felt doubly betrayed, firstly by the priest who 'befriended us when he arrived in Langdon,' and secondly by the Church for allowing him to come when it was clear there had been complaints about him before he left Ireland. He urged parents in Ireland to talk to their children, especially if they had been altar boys when Fr Smyth was in charge; it was vital if the priest was to be removed from society and put into prison where justice would prevent him from causing more pain. 'This man must be kept out of the priesthood because of the many lives he has ruined,' he said. 'How many families *has* he ruined; how many people's *faith* has he ruined? The man has done a lot of damage to a lot of people and I would like to see the children of Ireland and the children of North Dakota who have been molested to please come forward so that we the adults can do what has to be done to keep people like this off the streets and away from our children.'

For Bill, the most disgusting aspect of the whole affair was the fact that Fr Smyth had offended in Ireland long before he came to the United States and that, he said, raised the question about exactly how much the Church authorities knew. A fair question in the circumstances and one which was on my lips as I set off for Ireland, armed with the documentary evidence which would damn not only the paedophile priest, but those responsible for allowing him to travel to the United States in the first place when knowledge of his perversion had clearly been reported many times to a number of Church authorities. Fr Smyth had attempted to keep the lid on the abuse he inflicted on Dave by making payments to him but the act of making the payments was evidently not meant to be interpreted as anything more than an acknowledgement that he had molested Dave. As Dave said, the priest 'has not made any attempt to apologise.' Fr Smyth has a great deal to answer for but then so too have some individuals in the Church. As the plane took off from Minneapolis for the journey to London I knew it was almost the time to start asking the Church authorities who knew what and more importantly, when did they know it ... ?

7

Pursuit of the Truth

Author: Jim, when is ... when am I going to stop getting shunted about between the Abbey and the Church because somebody is going to stop passing the buck and make a decision about how you deal with this?.
Jim Cantwell: Yeah, well hold on now ...
Author: I think that's fair ...
Jim Cantwell: Yeah, that's fair but you're not a protagonist in the case, you're a journalist ... you have to sustain a certain detachment ...

Conversation with Jim Cantwell, director of the Catholic Church press office, Dublin.

Within ten days of arriving back from Minneapolis I was heading west in the direction of the United States again, this time on the narrow twisting roads that lead to the west coast of Ireland. It was Grand National day and I spent most of the journey thinking about placing a bet. It is the only time of the year I have a flutter. I kept telling myself to place a bet in the next town but of course I never placed that bet, preferring instead to keep moving towards the coast to meet John, the man who had rung me at home that morning. The call took me completely by surprise, for I had been told he was the one person abused by the priest who would never speak out.

My Saturday routine was given up the moment I spoke to him; it was a case of abandoning everything, putting the golf clubs away and hurriedly rearranging my schedule so I could be with John before nightfall. This was another breakthrough in the Fr Smyth story which was by now developing very positively. From slow beginnings, the pace with which this jigsaw puzzle was fitting together had quickened towards an almost complete picture of the events which were about to bring a Catholic priest before a court in Northern Ireland for child sex offences committed over three decades. During this time Fr Smyth had successfully evaded detection by the forces of justice. I had already met people who had been abused by the priest in the seventies and the eighties but John's story had a special significance; he claimed that Fr Smyth had abused him in the sixties and at the same time he was abusing his brother Anthony, the same Anthony who had broken the news about Fr Smyth to Bernie and Seamus in November 1988. As yet, there was no promise of an interview with John but I was prepared to make this long journey on the basis that it is much easier to determine the sincerity and truthfulness of someone face-to-face than it is over the telephone and it would provide both of us with an opportunity to form impressions about each other.

From my vantage point in one of the bay windows of the bar I could observe the hotel entrance and still enjoy a magnificent view as I sipped a pint of Guinness. It was not going to be difficult to spot John's arrival as there were few people in the bar, just a couple of refugees from a wedding reception who were in extremely animated form, gulping 'quickies' and laughing loudly at one another's jokes.

John apologised for being a few minutes late, explaining that he had been doing the Lotto. We ordered pints and began a journey into his past which served only to confirm the priest's methods. Soon we were becoming as animated as the wedding refugees and forging a bond of friendship which has outlasted the Fr Smyth television documentary. The word incongruous comes to mind to describe my situation as we chatted because ultimately my job was to ascertain from John details of the secret he had held within himself for most of his life, in fact for nearly two decades. He had opened up his heart to a detective from the RUC, prompted by the fact that other members of his family, his brother and four cousins, had done likewise. When he finally got around to the subject of the priest, after he had taken time to make his own assessment of me, he appeared to have a most understanding disposition, considering the circumstances of his life, which had been plagued by a variety of traumas because of the actions of Fr Smyth.

He was born in February 1960 and grew up with his brothers and sister in West Belfast in a caring family environment. His parents worked hard to provide for their children, to make sure they had not only normal comforts but the little extras which make childhood more pleasant. Fr Smyth was a regular caller at their home for as long as John could recall. He was also a friend of neighbours in the same street, like Sally and her sister, whose lives he had also touched. As in the other homes in the street which he visited, Fr Smyth would use horseplay with the children as a cover for his desire to fondle in a sexual manner, even managing to make these sexual advances right under the noses of loving parents who had no reason to doubt a man of the cloth. One might argue that John came into contact with the priest only because Fr Smyth was a personal friend of his parents. It is also possible to turn that on its head and say he was targeted by Fr Smyth because he was at an age where it would be in the priest's interests to engineer a friendship with the family.

John told me he first encountered Fr Smyth in the sixties when the priest began arriving at the family home. Initially he abused John's brother before turning his attentions to the youngest male of the household and, as the family learned only recently, also sexually abused the sister. It was a classic Fr Smyth violation not only of three children but of the family as well. John recognises that the reason for his silence for so many years was the guilt he felt and the realisation that if he had sought help and tried to expose the actions of the priest not only would he have had difficulty in finding someone to believe him but he would also have brought shame on his family. John said he would sometimes run off on seeing the priest approach the house but confessed that he could not do this on every occasion for fear of raising suspicions within the family. He reasoned it was better to stay and tolerate the sexual abuse which accompanied the horseplay rather than risk bringing disgrace on his family. That childhood judgement is characteristic of John today: an intelligent, caring person who ascribes two broken marriages to the baggage of pain he carries from what should have been his years of innocence.

'I tried to avoid him,' said John, 'but it was not always possible; you'd be caught unawares, sitting at home when he would walk in and begin the horseplay, clowning around. Maybe put his arm around me and bring me to another room; and it is like you do not call out to whoever is there that you don't want this happening or even to say "Help me!"Many a time you do feel like shouting but it is not that easy; and to understand that you have to be an abused person. You know what way people are going to react anyway. If you do say something, are they going to believe you, or are you going to get shouted at, scolded. So where do you cry for help and especially with a priest in your home which is a very respectable thing? He is a very trusted member of the family, so as a child you think to yourself am I going to be believed? What are they thinking is happening? So you just hope that one day it will go away.'

For John two failed marriages are a testimony to the fact that it did not just 'go away'. For seventeen years he tried to carry on living as normal, concealing the fact of his abuse by this priest, a priest who had the gall to turn up at one of his weddings. During that time he tried to get on with his life but always he had the feeling inside that the shame of what the priest had done was his, that he in some way had brought it upon himself. He finally broke his silence in 1992. The first person to hear John's story was a detective from the team set up to investigate the priest. The stigma of what happened in his childhood persists today.

Up to this point, John's story was confirmation of the methods Fr Smyth used to target children, but towards the end of the evening, John revealed an even darker side of the priest's behaviour. On trips away from home, approved of by unsuspecting parents, Fr Smyth would engage in a different type of sexual activity. The priest would sometimes take three or four children from different families on special journeys in his car for a weekend or a few days. John told me that when the priest got a group away all to himself he would sometimes force them into committing acts of sexual misconduct. 'I was on trips where he got me and another boy together in a room at an hotel or boarding-house,' John recalled, 'and he would force us to lie together on a bed while he watched us masturbate each other.' Unfortunately, when relating this tale to the police John could not identify the other boy as he thought he came from Dublin or somewhere else in the Republic. Some of the children would then be expected to mastur-bate the priest or be masturbated by him. No doubt others involved in such activity may yet decide to talk to the authorities about this as the investigation into Fr Smyth appears to have taken on a life of its own since his conviction and imprisonment.

From John I learned how Fr Smyth cast his baleful shadow over yet another life. This is the kind of turmoil that the victims of paedophiles usually suffer. From the outset I was aware of the need for sensitivity, realising that a reporter poking around in these disrupted lives could also stir up emotions and unwanted recollections. I did not seek lurid descriptions of abuse; that was left to the individual to decide for himself or herself. I was determined that whatever the individual sitting on the other side of the camera would be prepared to put on record, the *Counterpoint* programme was not going to be salacious, although by its nature there would inevitably be an element of voyeurism.

What has brought John safely through all the crises in his short life is his will to fight back against the odds, although it is only recently that he has begun to receive counselling to help him cope with those lonely moments when the past creeps into the present. That he is finally seeking help springs from his own determination to overcome the grief Fr Smyth introduced to his life and not from any effort by the Church authorities to provide him with assistance. Even when he met two senior members of the Norbertine Order in mid-September last year they offered him no help. Former Abbot Kevin Smith and Fr Gerard Cusack, appointed administrator at Kilnacrott when the Abbot resigned, listened to John's story and offered their assurances that a special committee had been set up to deal with cases of Fr Smyth's abuse. During these conversations they told him that the Church had long ago recognised and identified the problem of alcoholism but paedophilia was a new dilemma. However, in common with many other institutions in society, the Church was rapidly coming to terms with and learning how to proceed when it came to dealing with a paedophile priest. They knew from experience how to deal with alcoholics; now they were dealing with what they referred to as the world of 'sexaholics'. Whatever these procedures may be, they appear at this stage not to include any programme of assistance, financial or otherwise, for the people most hurt by their priest.

John still endures sleepless nights, nightmares and a growing uncertainty about his past, most particularly his childhood. In a moment of despair he tried to find verbal expression for that intangible pain – the pain which he regrets inflicting on those around him who had love in their hearts. What he wrote is as much an expression of his sorrow at their suffering as it is about his own pain:

8.30 pm Feeling lonely and depressed, suicidal, looking for a turning-point in my emotions. There seems to be no crossroads to change direction as I feel I have travelled all the roads. Looking at the end of the road, dead end. Grass or sea? Looks inviting, cold but could be warm on the other side. I want to be taken. Taken now! Released to the person I should be, not what I'm trying to be, or not what other people expect me to be. Still feeling lonely! No escape – only my thoughts to battle with; they seem to be winning. Head rules the heart – heart rules the head. No laws when it comes to love. Love goes! Empty feeling – fill the gap, with what? Work? Play? Friends? Everywhere I go the answer is still no. No replacement for love. You strip me to the bone. No turning point in my thoughts. Every-thing leads in one direction. *Abuse*, I scream; it all leads in one direction. Escape, maybe for a night or two but the direction is still waiting for you. *Help!* Still feeling lonely. Could fight the world with the anger I feel but to no avail as my ammunition is blank. No thought, no direction. *Christ!* Where have I been? So out of touch, somebody help me. I'm not drained; I look that way. What would you do or what would you say? When someone puts a syringe into your system and drains away – without thought or care, please realise ... *Oh stop!* How much do you want? My feelings may be an ocean but don't leave me with this stream. *Please go away!*

Apart from my unexpected meeting with John, Saturday, 9 April 1994 was significant for another reason. Earlier that morning I had taken the first step in seeking to hear the other side of the story by contacting Abbot Kevin Smith at Kilnacrott Abbey in Ballyjamesduff. He told me he was aware of Fr Smyth's difficulties with the police in Northern Ireland but could not possibly agree at this stage to doing an interview. In any case, he said he had been instructed to seek formal written requests for interviews from reporters. This is how the conversation progressed at this point:

Author: Why do you need it in writing?
Abbot Smith: We were told just to get it in writing.
Author: Who told you?
Abbot Smith: No, it doesn't count now, OK?
Author: I'll certainly give it to you in writing.
Abbot Smith: OK, good, OK.

My request was transferred from the oral to the written, and anxious to ensure its safe arrival at Holy Trinity Abbey I drove to Ballyjamesduff myself on Monday, 11 April. I never did get my interview or even a chat with the Abbot. In fact for the next five months I got the runaround from representatives of the Catholic Church and the Norbertine Order, who could not bring themselves to face television cameras or show public accountability for the deeds of a priest who had abused children for decades.

As those abused suffered and struggled to keep a hold on reality, the abuser got on with his life, preaching Christian values, listening to sinners in confession and signing Mass cards wherever he went to support his comfortable lifestyle. He enjoyed the respect and admiration of a society which afforded him privileges in keeping with his position in the community. He was free to travel anywhere in the world with the reputation of a man of virtue and, in spite of his vow of poverty, he always seemed to have funds to buy new cars. Indeed, as I discovered in Cavan, at one stage Fr Smyth's financial status attracted the attention of local gardai curious to discover his source of funding. My source says little was learned from their investigations other than that he seemed to make a tidy sum from signing Mass cards in a couple of shops in the area.

Behind him he left a trail of human misery, broken marriages and suicide attempts. Five of the people involved in the court action against Fr Smyth experienced the trauma of broken marriages, three attempted suicide, one of them six times. This was the human side of the Fr

Smyth story and it was being told to us by people who wanted television to assist them in their quest for justice and public vindication of their actions. Most important of all, they wanted the Church to take public responsibility for the behaviour of its members, members of the clergy who had shielded a paedophile and were then prepared to try and cover up the fact they had failed to act. The complainants were ordinary Catholic people, who through sheer frustration at the attitude of the Church authorities felt compelled to put their own, or more importantly their children's, interests first and the welfare of the Church second, people who were now, as a last resort, seeking voice through the medium of broadcasting.

Twenty-five years experience of reporting the conflict in a divided community taught me to differentiate between truth and perception. I realised that to secure the 'truth and nothing but the truth' was an ideal not always achievable since reporters must respond to events and depend on second- or third-hand versions of this 'truth'. Facts are facts and it is essential in the interests of natural justice to report both sides of the story, to represent the 'facts' as viewed from opposite positions. My telephone call to Abbot Kevin Smith on 9 April 1994 had began the process of seeking out the other side of the story. From the outset he was unhelpful and in that first conversation I asked a question to which, as he was eventually to admit himself, he gave me an untruthful answer:

Author: Do you have a Fr Marshall there?
Abbot: Yes.
Author: A Fr Bernard Marshall?

Abbot: Yes, yes.

Author: Has he been ringing some of the families of the victims?

Abbot: Not that I know of . . .

Author: On behalf of the Church . . . .?

Abbot: Not that I know of; no.

Author: He hasn't?

Abbot: No.

Author: Do you know of a Fr Marshall who's been ringing the families of victims offering them financial assistance?

Abbot: We . . . he would, he would be a friend of them; he would be ringing them as a friend.

Author: Sorry?

Abbot: He would be ringing them as he is a friend of the family.

Author: They don't seem to know him.

Abbot: Ah, of course they know him.

Author: One of them doesn't . . .

Abbot: He lived beside them.

The Abbot was not in touch with me for some months. It was not until September 1994 that he finally made an admission about Fr Marshall. This is what he said in a fax sent on the twenty-sixth of that month, just ten days before we planned to transmit our programme:

With my approval, in December, 1993, Fr Marshall, one of our community, telephoned the father of one of the young people against whom Fr Smyth had offended. Our purpose was to arrange a meeting with the young person's father to discuss Fr Smyth's offending and its possible consequences for the victim and the community.

There in black and white Abbot Smith owned up to an untruth and, aside from the obvious fact that he declined an opportunity to tell me the truth on 9 April, there are two other very simple observations to make. Firstly, in the initial call I did not name the persons to whom I was referring, who happen to be Bernie and Seamus, and when I told Seamus what the Abbot said about Fr Marshall telephoning him because he knew him, he responded: 'Listen, I know you better than I know him. I would not know him if I fell over him in the street.' I pointed out that the Abbot said the only reason Fr Marshall called him was because he was a friend. 'I would have a better idea of my friends than the Abbot and Fr Marshall is no friend of mine.'

Secondly, in his statement the Abbot does not identify the family I was alluding to but what he does do is to clearly identify the month and year of the call. December 1993 was a bad month for Bernie and Seamus: their daughter Susan made an unsuccessful attempt on her life. They had very good reason to recall exactly the timing of Fr Marshall's contact because it came shortly after Susan had attempted to take her own life. It was Seamus who took the call, but in answer to my question regarding 'financial assistance' he wants it to be made clear there was no such offer to him from Fr Marshall. It is noticeable that this question was the first to bring the Abbot to admit there had been calls from Fr Marshall. The reason I had mentioned 'financial assistance' in the first place was because of a conversation I had with a community worker in West Belfast who made me aware that Fr Marshall had been making calls to families in her area.

According to Seamus, Fr Marshall had another reason for making the call. 'I received a phone call from a friend of Fr Smyth, Fr Marshall, and the man was quite insistent that he come to speak to me. I told him that I had nothing I wished to talk to him about and I would not want a priest in my home at the moment; it just wasn't on as far as I was concerned. The call lasted about twenty to twenty-five minutes in which time Fr Marshall's attitude was that Fr Smyth was a good priest, a man who had done much good work. I don't deny that he did, but as far as I am concerned the bad outweighs the good. He said people in the abbey wouldn't like what I had done. If we were to meet, perhaps another means could be found to deal with Fr Smyth which would not involve the police or any action in the courts. When I complained that what he was suggesting was protecting a criminal, he went into a temper. I finished the conversation at this point.'

Bernie and Seamus were in no mood for any kind of compromise; in their opinion that opportunity had long since been passed up by Fr Smyth's friends at the abbey in Ballyjamesduff. After months of anxiety following Anthony's confrontation with Fr Smyth in 1989, they had approached Abbot Smith and arranged a meeting at an hotel in Armagh. It lasted for an hour, during which time they told the Abbot of the enormity of the breach of trust by Fr Smyth, that four of their children had been abused by the priest and they wanted to know what action the abbey would take. The Abbot listened politely, taking notes, but offered little by way of comfort and certainly no promise of action. 'The Abbot admitted that he had complaints about Fr Smyth as far back as 1970,' Seamus recalled, 'and Bernie pointed out to him that our children were not even born then. He said he assumed he was cured and explained he could not really curtail the priest's movements as he was a grown man and was free to move wherever he wanted.' Seamus told me he had suggested a solution. 'We even asked the Abbot if Fr Smyth could be put into an enclosed religious order so that he would not be near any other children but he said no, he could not do that.'

The Abbot told them Fr Smyth was a 'loner' at the abbey where he ate on his own and sat alone. Then he mentioned his disapproval of some of the literature the priest read, something which had been found in his room, although he declined to elaborate on exactly what he meant. The Belfast couple left the Armagh hotel to drive home, totally dissatisfied with what they had been told. Seamus explained: 'He was a bit offhand when we asked how he would deal with the problem; it was more or less that Fr Smyth had got treatment and he assumed that this treatment had cured him, and if we could just run along home he would get more treatment, so just go on home and forget about it. All he had wanted from us was information about Fr Smyth's movements and he just did not give the impression at all of caring one iota about the problems we had at home because of Fr Smyth.' So that appeared to be that as far as Abbot Smith was concerned. But if this is how Abbot Smith had dealt with complaints in the past, he was mistaken if he thought this would be sufficient to rid himself of Bernie and Seamus. In any event, he did not feel there was need for further contact – at least until he organised the call from Fr Marshall in December 1993. Of course by then he was aware that Bernie and Seamus were rocking the boat: they had gone to the police and Fr Smyth was on the run, hiding out in the abbey.

While Abbot Smith considered my request in consultation with whoever had instructed him to get it in writing, there were other approaches to be made to get an understanding of the Church's position. Two days after my visit to Kilnacrott Abbey, I contacted Jim Cantwell, director of the Catholic press office in Dublin. I outlined the situation, and he redirected me towards the abbey at Kilnacrott. He said the Church took very seriously the problem of child sex-abuse not only by the clergy but by anyone. He reminded me that sex abuse of children had only emerged as a problem in the past ten years, not just in Ireland but throughout the world. Mr Cantwell referred to a report in 1980 by the Department of Health in the Republic which did not mention child sex-abuse, but in 1987 when another report was produced guidelines were laid down which, he said, the Church was following. In the meantime, the bishops and major religious superiors were holding a series of seminars on the whole question of sex abuse covering all aspects – civil, legal, pastoral, psychological and spiritual – with a view to producing guidelines for dealing with a problem 'which unfortunately pervades all sections of society'. He went on: 'Sex abuse is an appalling event at any time, but it has a particular thing when people who are placed in positions of trust over young people are involved and that . . . for example, would be parents where it ... ah..ah ... most of the sexual abuse goes on, but it also includes priests, where there is a particularly deep breach of trust.'

Moving swiftly from the complexities of sexual abuse in society, Mr Cantwell raised the question of Church protocol. I should first understand the structure of the Catholic Church. In my ignorance I had assumed the Church was ultimately responsible for the behaviour of all priests in Ireland, whether or not they belonged to religious orders. The Catholic families I had been dealing with were under the same impression. Like the families, I believed the buck stopped with the Primate, Cardinal Cahal Daly, the man presented publicly as the head of the Catholic Church in Ireland. This was a misconception apparently, because according to Mr Cantwell, Cardinal Daly's authority was confined to the Archdiocese of Armagh where he is archbishop. Matters relating to a priest from a religious order were the business of the religious superior of the order. But, I asked, what about a situation where a priest from an order commits offences whilst in a diocese, as Fr Smyth had in Down and Connor. The answer was that because he was not on official pastoral duty the bishop still had no authority to discipline him; he could do no more than contact the religious superior to register a complaint and to request action. (It would eventually become clear that he had occasion to do just that.) By the end of our conversation I was convinced the Church was attempting to put a safe distance between itself and Fr Smyth. As the next few months went by I regularly called the abbey and Jim Cantwell in the hope that at some stage I would find somebody prepared to answer the questions about Fr Smyth.

The impression I received was that the Church was washing its hands of Fr Smyth by telling me that the only person who could deal with my questions was the religious superior of Fr Smyth's order, Abbot Kevin Smith. Abbot Smith, meanwhile, was refusing to answer questions and kept referring to his legal advisers who, he said, would determine whether or not I would get an interview – although he thought I would. At one stage he told me I would be getting a letter from his legal advisers and was in fact surprised I had not yet received that communication. It never arrived. I was faced with a situation in which no one seemed to be prepared to put his head above the parapet to explain how a paedophile priest could be allowed to continue to abuse for more than thirty years even though there had been complaints made to the Catholic authorities in Belfast. I was still of the view that this was a problem for the Church and not just for Fr Smyth's Norbertine Order.

As time went on I was concerned that this story would go out without any input from the Catholic Church and I wanted to be sure that everyone was aware that I had done my best to secure an interview with someone from the Church to explain the Fr Smyth story from their perspective. Basically, I suppose I still had not come to terms with the niceties of canon v. civil law and was left with the distinct impression that whatever view the Church was taking of the Fr Smyth affair, it was being taken in some kind of isolation from that of the Norbertine Order's headquarters in County Cavan. The result was confusion on my part, confusion because it was difficult to believe that somehow the Catholic Church version of the story was possibly going to go by default. The Church appeared to be pushing the order further and further out of reach, leaving it to accept the full blame for what had been going on, isolating the Abbot and his community from the main body of the Church.

After weeks of calls the Catholic Church was finally prepared to put someone up for interview, but only on the basis that he was not asked specifically about Fr Smyth. The interviewee would take part only to answer questions on the wider issue of the positive action being taken by the Church to deal with the problem of paedophile priests. Of course we were interested in hearing that view, but as far as we were concerned, the Church still had a moral responsibility to face up to the issue of Fr Smyth. I kept pushing for an explanation, as the following exchange with Jim Cantwell illustrates.

Author: There seems to be a lot of confusion here Jim, right . . . .

Jim Cantwell: Yeah . . .

Author: I have spoken to the Abbot of Kilnacrott . . . I'm assured that I'll receive a letter in writing and I'm assured that he will do an interview . . .

Jim Cantwell: Hum . . .

Author: But I think it's a bit, if you've been enquiring into this or have been asking people to talk about it or to give a . . .

Jim Cantwell: No, no, no . . .

Author: . . . a wider perspective, what's confusing me

is I'm getting bounced along here by, I mean it doesn't really matter to me at the end of the day because, I mean, I've got a programme and I've got enough information that will, I mean it's not going to look good for you guys if you don't face up to it. I mean, I'm, I'm ...

Jim Cantwell: Yeah. Well, hold on now Chris ... what I'll ... when we were talking, what you wanted was somebody who would talk about the overall thing, not about a specific case, isn't that right?

Author: Yes, that's right and I have specific questions to ask of the Catholic Church through you as their press officer, questions relating to Fr Smyth's behaviour and the demeanour of the people who handled and looked after him.

Jim Cantwell: Yeah, well I now have you ... you, the, the, the Abbot has agreed to talk to you about that.

Author: Well, he's agreed but he hasn't thus far ... he's said that I will get a letter in writing which I haven't yet received, ah, so I don't know what exactly is going on ... anyway, the point of it is there are serious questions to be asked about why this man was able to move around the Catholic Church, whether or not he's a member of the Catholic Church or an order, and you keep pointing me towards an order, the point about it is, these offences took place in properties not run by the order ... in schools in Belfast for example. Are you aware of this?

Jim Cantwell: I'm not aware of the details of the case, no. I haven't, I'm not aware of the details of the case at all ...

Author: Well, Jim I think . . .

Jim Cantwell: I haven't seen the charges . . .

Author: Well, Jim I think you should have a long chat with somebody because these are questions. I'm not going to be the only one who is going to be asking these, it's about time the Church took it seriously . . .

Jim Cantwell: Well no . . . hold on now . . . hold on . . .

Author: These are offences which took place on Church property . . .

Jim Cantwell: Hold on now, hold on Chris for a second, the Church is taking it seriously . . .

Author: . . . plummeting the depths of thirty years of abuse.

Jim Cantwell: I am aware of the seriousness of it, don't get me wrong.

Author: I'm, when is . . . when am I going to stop getting shunted about between the abbey and the Church because somebody somewhere is going to stop passing the buck and make a decision about how you deal with this?

Jim Cantwell: Yeah, well, now, hold on . . .

Author: I think that's fair . . .

Jim Cantwell: Yeah, that's fair but you're not a protagonist in the case, you're a journalist . . . you have to sustain a certain detachment . . .

Author: Sure . . .

Jim Cantwell: But what I'm saying to you, I'm considering the matter as serious as I can and expeditiously as I can but I can do no more at this stage.

It was to be some time before I was to learn the truth of

what was going on behind the scenes and only after transmission of our programme on Fr Smyth in October 1994. But if the Catholic Church had difficulties talking about Fr Smyth during preparations for that broadcast, members of the Church who had been abused by the priest had no such difficulty in speaking out. As the summer of 1994 approached I was given a tip by what journalists often describe as 'an informed source' who pointed me in the direction of a woman in her thirties, someone he said, with a particularly moving story to tell. Nothing I had heard up to now prepared me for what she had to say.

8

TURN AWAY. DON'T LOOK AT ME.

Overdose

I seem to always
Try to end my life;
All these years it's been a strife.
I still see that awful face
And remember what took place.

How will I ever get free
And try to find the real me?
Is it always to remain
Time after time in my brain.

How can a child know what went on
Or even know that it was wrong?
Now you can see why I don't want to live,
'Cause all these things I can't forgive.
A man of God did this to me,
An overdose would surely set me free.

(Written on 21 October 1994 by Siobhan, who was sexually abused by Fr Smyth for eight years after being placed in care in a Catholic orphanage in Belfast)

Siobhan was just six years of age when her mother ended her life with an overdose leaving six children alone in the world without a mother and abandoned by their father. (A seventh child had died years earlier in his cot.) Two of the six were placed with relatives but Siobhan was one of the remaining four placed in care at Nazareth House on the Ormeau Road in South Belfast. They would say there was little love shown to those unfortunate enough to find themselves, through no fault of their own, living behind the high red brick walls of this orphanage. Siobhan, her sisters Marie and Angela, and her brother Danny were all abused by Fr Brendan Smyth whilst in care. Angela has not been traced since she told her story on RTE radio in October 1994 in spite of the best efforts of the RUC. In any event, Fr Smyth seemed to have had unlimited access to them, just as he had at Catholic schools in the city. Their story is one of the most touching and horrific in the Fr Smyth dossier.

Siobhan, who is now thirty-three years old and the mother of four children of her own, remembers that she and Danny remained together at Nazareth House for about six months. Her sisters Marie (four years older) and Angela (three years older) were moved within a matter of weeks to the Good Shepherd establishment, just a few yards away on the opposite side of the Ormeau Road. During that first six months Fr Smyth began calling at Nazareth House to see them although Siobhan cannot be sure why he showed any interest in them unless perhaps it stemmed from some kind of friendship or relationship he had with her older sister Marie. As far as she remembers Fr Smyth was not a friend of her family prior to the break-up of the family unit and it is interesting to note that in singling out members of Siobhan's family, Fr Smyth was actually breaking away from his normal pattern which was to establish friendship with the parents of those he had designs on.

In her home today Siobhan proudly has on display a framed certificate for ballet obtained during her time in Nazareth House, but it is her only happy memory of a place she grew to detest. Every time she looks at the certificate on the mantelpiece she enjoys the warmth of the memory of participation in expressive dancing but it is undoubtedly tempered by the other painful memories it evokes. Siobhan recalls meeting Fr Smyth for the first time during the first week that she and her brother Danny were alone in the orphanage, after her two sisters had been moved to the home across the road. At first Fr Smyth was, to use her word, 'sweet' to them, showing what they mistook at the time for kindness but which they now realise was the method applied by the priest to target them for abuse, and the abuses were not far away. He returned the following week and again was provided with a room in which to spend time with Siobhan and Danny, although on this occasion he simply chatted to them, making them feel wanted in what was still a strange, unfriendly environment for them. Fr Smyth discovered that Siobhan attended her ballet classes once a week, on

Tuesdays as she recalls, and the next week he made it his business to arrive on the day Siobhan was at ballet class.

In his clerical clothing Fr Smyth was apparently always welcome at Nazareth House; the nuns who ran the home did not, it seems, question his relationship with Siobhan and Danny. On Tuesdays the priest arrived at the orphanage around 4.30 pm or 5 pm and was shown directly into a room reserved for visitors, where he would be provided with a cup of tea. Danny would be brought to him and once they were left alone and undisturbed sexual abuses would take place. Around six o'clock Siobhan would arrive back from ballet and Danny would be despatched to his room while his sister was taken to the visitor's room to be alone with Fr Smyth. He would immediately instruct her to remove her school skirt to reveal her ballet outfit underneath and he would then ask her to parade in front of him, listening to his constant prompts to walk away from him without looking around. Sometimes he would ignore this ritual and would simply tell Siobhan to pull up her school skirt as he had done on the first occasion they were alone in the room. This is how Siobhan recalled that first encounter.

I came home from ballet and I had my leotard on and I had my school skirt and he says to me, 'Pull your skirt up.' I was sort of scared and didn't know what to do and he says, 'I told you to pull your skirt up.' So I pulled my skirt up and he says to me, 'What colour knickers have you got on?' and I told him the colour and then he said, 'Come over and sit on my knee.' So I came over and sat on his knee and he put me on his leg and started shaking it so his hand kept going up and up my leg and he ... I kept looking at him and he says, 'Turn your head and don't look at me.' So I was just sitting there and I was scared. I was crying and then he started putting his hands up my knickers and then up into my vagina.

I told him to stop it, so then he just kept on doing that there and then ... he put ... he put his hand up, his fingers up my back passage and that, but he never touched me at the top, it was always at the bottom he did it.

To put this in context, Fr Smyth in just a few minutes had ruined the life of an innocent young girl. He left a bewildered and hurt child with a hymen broken by his masturbation. He had obtained sexual gratification from anal and vaginal penetration. Fighting back tears, Siobhan said this abuse continued every week for eight years even though, she says, she complained to one of the nuns. When I asked what reaction this complaint drew, Siobhan said:

She ripped the hair out of me and beat me on the head, over the head, with a bunch of keys and made me kneel outside the door all night and pray. You know I was scared to tell after that. I just had to sit there when he came and let him do what he was doing because she'd have killed me.

Throughout all this, Siobhan says, Fr Smyth talked 'sweetly' when they were alone, promising all kinds of trips away in his car for weekends or outings to the cinema although he would raise his voice if she tried to look at him while the abuses were taking place.

Siobhan was vulnerable, lonely, afraid and bewildered because of her mother's sudden death when she arrived at Nazareth House in need of love, care and affection. That she got punished for complaining is something she can never forget because she had no one else to turn to for help, not even her social worker whom she feared would report the conversation, leaving her to face further punishment once he had gone. It is almost impossible to imagine the misery in Siobhan's life at this time. It found expression in misbehaviour or by running away and yet no one attempted to understand or find out the reason for her unsettled personality. Siobhan put this behaviour down to the fact that 'mummy died, and I did not want to tell them the truth because, eh, just to please them. My mummy took an overdose and killed herself but I used to always make an excuse that it was because of her I was doing this and then they sent me to a psychiatrist and then I told him the same too. I just didn't want anyone to know about mummy.' So as she struggled to deal with her mother's death, for one hour every week for eight years Siobhan endured the touch of a man who pretended to be friendly and kind but who in fact was inflicting deeper psychological wounds on the child.

Fearing the consequences of any attempt to report Fr Smyth, Siobhan said she ran away from the home over a hundred times, went so far as to take overdoses of drugs and once even tried to slit her wrists. When she was fourteen she was sent to Middletown Convent in County Armagh, where her sister Marie spent some time prior to

Siobhan's arrival. As far as Siobhan was concerned this training school was the closest she had come to having a home life. The quality of her life improved dramatically the moment she got out of Nazareth House, rescued by a court order sending her to the convent for three years. Siobhan said the nuns here were genuinely kind, compassionate and helpful; gone were the days of feeling unloved, unwanted and above all feeling betrayed by those who were supposed to have a responsibility to care but who seemed to go out of their way to demonstrate the exact opposite.

Siobhan thought the move to County Armagh had finally broken the link with Fr Smyth, that for the first time in eight years she was free from sexual abuse. The joy at the thought of not having to see the priest again was shortlived. She recalls the day she was told a priest was coming to see her, a friend of the family who apparently had been a regular visitor at Nazareth House. Siobhan says she was petrified at the thought of having to entertain the priest again and such was her distress at the prospect of being alone with him that she somehow found the courage to tell staff she did not want to be left alone with him, that she did not like him. She did not say the priest had been abusing her and the nun did not ask any questions but assured Siobhan that someone would accompany her for the duration of the priest's visit.

Fr Smyth was led into a room to see Siobhan but this time the nun who had brought him from reception remained, leaving briefly only to make a cup of tea and making sure the door into the kitchen was left open at all times, even remarking to Siobhan as she left, 'If you need me call me.' In the absence of the opportunity to continue his sexual assaults, the priest's conversation with Siobhan was decidedly muted. It was as if he realised he had been rumbled and that no matter how long he waited there was not going to be any time alone with her. He reached out his hand to present the girl with the bag of sweets he brought on every visit as he waited for tea to be served. They were eaten in an uneasy silence as Siobhan had nothing to communicate to the man she despised and the nun simply maintained a presence so that the child's wishes would be honoured. Once he had finished his tea and biscuits the priest stood up to say his farewells to Siobhan, wishing her well and squeezing a five-pound note into her hand as he made his way to the door. It was the last time Siobhan saw him, until that day in January 1994, when he appeared on the television screen.

Siobhan had a familiar tale to tell as she described how she had made contact with the team of detectives investigating the priest. She will never forget what Fr Smyth has done to her but has tried to make her own way through life, trying to push the horrible memories to the back of her mind. After years of existing without having to face the priest, suddenly his face and eyes sought her out as she was watching television at a friend's house; the date was 21 January 1994.

TV Face

Sitting in the house
Watching TV. Nobody
Around, just the child and me.
I seen [sic] Smyth's face appearing on TV.
He is coming, he is coming,
Coming to get me.
I was frightened; I was scared.
I ran out with fright
To see who I could see to start a fight.
I ran to the phone and rang CID.
They came out to see if they could help me.
They listen to my story,
As I began to speak.
All I could think: he was such a creep,
The things he done, the things he said,
Kept going round in my head.
I went to the station,
Where I could explain.
They sat and listened,
As I went through it all again.
I felt good inside; I got it all out
The dark secret I tried to forget.

Siobhan, 14 October 1994

Just like Sally and Sarah, Siobhan was stung into action
when she saw Fr Smyth's image on the teatime news as
he came out of a court building in Belfast. She was in a
neighbour's house at the time and once she caught sight

of him she says she went 'mental', running out of the house screaming incoherently with her worried friend chasing behind, calling on her to return to the house. As part of her in-built will to put the past behind her, Siobhan had consciously decided not to tell anyone about the priest. But now with his face on television because others had stood up against him, she found a surge of courage flowing throw her body and immediately got in touch with her local police, who apparently spent something like three hours trying to calm her down. At last, though, someone was listening to her pained cry for help and was actually going to do something about it; at last there was a chance to make the priest pay for the life of silent suffering that she had had to endure. She made statements to detectives but it was only after she saw others having the courage finally to unburden themselves of the guilt the priest left in all those he abused that she was prepared to make the move herself.

When detectives confronted Fr Smyth with Siobhan's story about Nazareth House he admitted visiting the establishment and told them there was a 'visitor's room' which he used. When asked if he remembered being there with any young girls he gave another rambling reply: 'If by that you mean do I get aroused when I see somebody like that, you know, or if I'm in the company of somebody like that not necessarily at all. But I'm just . . . this is the way I can explain it. I'm not a medical person and I feel it would give me pleasure to fondle maybe this one or that one but not necessarily everyone.' Just one of the many confusing answers Fr Smyth gave police during many hours of questioning. When confronted on the issue of 'digital penetration' Fr Smyth denied doing this, although at his trial he pleaded guilty to all seventeen charges, including those based on the statements made by Siobhan.

(Untitled poem)

All my life I've been abused.
Still today I feel used;
No one knows the pain I bear
But then again, do they care?
Just a child of six years old,
No one listened when I told.
All the grief and all the pain,
A cry for help was all in vain.
Sitting alone here today
I wonder will he really pay,
Or is this all in vain.
Yet still I have to suffer the pain.
I now have children, four.
Lord above, I can take no more:
All I want is peace of mind
But it's so damned hard to find.
Every day brings something new,
I've learned to trust only a chosen few,
I pray to God and live in hope
To give me the strength so I can cope.

Siobhan, 11 October 1994

That poem was written just five days after Siobhan appeared in silhouette on *Suffer Little Children* on UTV, laying bare her suffering for the world to see. What is not immediately evident on the screen, since Siobhan's appearance is disguised and an actress is reading her words, is the immense pain felt when she is asked to think back to the days Fr Smyth made himself a part of her life. The actress did a magnificent voice-over of Siobhan's haunting account but no matter how gifted or competent a job it is impossible not to lose something in the translation necessary to make it safe for Siobhan to contribute to the programme. She says it has been impossible for her to establish a lasting relationship with a man and she points the finger of blame at the abuse she suffered from the unwanted attentions of Fr Smyth. With a sardonic smile Siobhan says people will find it strange that she has four children, all boys, when they learn she cannot bear a man's touch. Making love is something which has happened to her in attempts to sustain a relationship but in truth, and to use her own words, 'During sex I just lie there, rigid with fear.' Naturally, this frigidity places stress on relationships and as a consequence Siobhan has never fulfilled her dreams of normality, husband, children, mortgage and a decent life with a few extra pounds to spend. She is now in a trap with little in her life to encourage her to look forward to tomorrow with any confidence that it will be better than today. 'Maybe that is why I've tried to take my life six times,' she casually drops into the conversation. Christmas 1994 was spent in hospital and then a psychiatric unit where she had to plead to be allowed to leave because the authorities feared a repeat. Her whole life has been disrupted by the injustice and hurt caused by Fr Brendan Smyth.

Any hope Siobhan had that life would begin to approach normality was again shortlived. Not long after leaving the convent to begin life on her own, she was sexually abused by a relative. Recently she related this experience to the police, who may decide to take further action.

When they were separated in childhood Siobhan, her brother and two sisters lost track of one another, collectively unaware of the fact that Fr Smyth had been forcing his sexual advances on each of them individually. It has to be said, however, that each had suspicions they were not alone in being the object of the priest's unwanted attentions. In a perverse kind of logic, the public exposure of Fr Smyth as a paedophile brought them closer together again, giving them a common theme in their lives, an opportunity to seek support and help from within the shattered remains of their family. Siobhan's brother Danny was just four when his mother committed suicide in a Belfast hostel. The children were initially placed in Nazareth House but from there Danny was sent to another Catholic institution which cannot at this point be identified for legal reasons as it is under investigation by the police. He was eleven years of age and by this stage had already endured many years of abuse by the priest. His transfer to new surroundings did not bring about a cessation of the visits by Fr Smyth, who simply followed him there. As if this were not bad enough Danny was soon thrown into the worst period of his short life, facing sexual abuse on a grand scale, suffering painful degradation and humiliation by up to ten other priests, buggery by other boys in the residence, orchestrated and observed by some of the priests and group sex sessions with other boys led by, and again observed by, other priests.

One of the priests at this establishment was a friend of Fr Smyth and on the occasion of the monthly visits of the priest from Ballyjamesduff he would supply a number of boys for his guest's sexual amusement. Danny was just one of the boys told to report for private meetings with Fr Smyth, waiting in line outside the room set aside for these sessions. Danny told me other priests would tell him that, 'Fr Brendan is here to see you,' and if there was somebody in the designated room with him, simply to wait outside until called. As soon as he was alone with the priest the kissing would begin, not the fatherly peck on the cheek: French kissing with the priest's tongue probing the boy's mouth. Then the priest would open his trousers and place the boy's hand on his penis, making the boy masturbate him until he ejaculated. Once that had been achieved – and the sessions normally lasted for fifteen or twenty minutes – the boy would be quickly taken to the priest's car to receive a bag of sweets and a couple of pounds pocket money. The next boy would be called in for more of the same. For a boy of eleven years of age this was not only disgusting behaviour but it simply was not in keeping with the teachings of the Church: 'Masturbation was a sin,' said Danny. 'At least that is what we were told – although it seemed to be permitted if you were doing it to or with a priest.'

A few years later when Danny was fourteen or fifteen one of the priests at this establishment who regularly abused Danny once caught him with some other boys and a group of girls. Danny was kissing one of the girls when the priest came upon this 'horrific' scene. He was immediately ordered to stop and when he reported to an office for punishment he was caned and told that kind of behaviour was not acceptable; it was immoral and such depraved thoughts and deeds should be saved for marriage. Danny fears that a lasting relationship is doomed by his uncertainty about his partner's reaction to any revelation about his past.

Danny took the first opportunity afforded him to escape his living hell. It came with a move to England, out of the reach of Fr Brendan Smyth and the other perverted priests. Nowadays he refuses to enter churches of any kind; he feels he has been betrayed by the Catholic Church and by the priests in whose care he was placed when his family fell apart and he was in need of love and affection. Instead he lost his innocence and was forced to submit to sustained humiliating and degrading treatment which scarred him for life. As he bluntly puts it himself: 'The Catholic Church betrayed me and my family. Now I want justice. I want to see those responsible put on trial publicly and jailed for a very long time, perhaps for as many years as I have suffered.' Danny's story like all the others, is the human side of a major issue confronting society today, but it is these tales of suffering that the Church would prefer did not get a public airing. Danny was not the first of the abused to comment: 'As far as the Church is concerned we are expendable if it helps preserve it in a good light.' As events turned out, exposure of the dark corners of the Church produced scandal and serious questions about its management policy and public image.

9

THE BURDEN OF GUILT

I was never in the habit of sticking my fingers into anyone. I did it once to an adult, just to see what it felt like. It's not sexual intercourse.

Fr Brendan Smyth, 1994

The paradox of paedophilia is that it is the abused and not the abuser who experience the pain, suffer the degradation and ultimately carry the burden of guilt: paedophiles rarely feel culpability for their actions. For five decades Fr Brendan Smyth offended hundreds of times, in all probability, against hundreds of innocent children. Not only has he not shown any public remorse for his actions during time spent in private with those he abused; he has spurned opportunities to say he was sorry.

From what I have been able to learn about Fr Smyth's behaviour since his arrest and conviction it seems that throughout his interviews he maintained the same detached air he displayed in his everyday life when it suited him, keeping up his guard, and apparently not uttering one word of contrition. Court records will show that Fr Smyth eventually pleaded guilty to seventeen charges and was jailed for four years; but it is what the records don't show that will remain secret and deprive society of an understanding of the priest who abused children for more than forty years. The net effect of Fr Smyth admitting all the charges was to prevent a full ventilation of the facts of the case against him in open court, to deny the public an opportunity of learning the true extent of his career as a child sex molester. This situation clearly suited Fr Smyth and also suited the Catholic Church, in that it denied the case unwelcome publicity which would undoubtedly have embarrassed all those in the Church who had responsibility for him. In order to get away with his crimes for as long as he did, Fr Smyth had to develop a number of personalities, each one designed to match the company he was keeping. It was, therefore, never going to be an easy task to discover the real man.

There is no doubt the police profile of the priest would have provided an interesting insight into the mind of a paedophile, but those records are now carefully stored along with the court papers. My attempts to gain access to these records failed, although I did pick up one or two details along the way from a variety of disparate sources. Prison staff will also have had the opportunity to put together a picture of the priest and by drawing on the experiences of those who knew him well it is possible to make an educated guess at the kind of man who faced police officers across the interview table and who confronted prison staff.

It is clear that getting information from him was a cat-and-mouse game. He made no attempt to co-operate, giving rambling, often nonsensical, answers. The skilled interviewing officers could, however, often draw from them clues about real motivations and edge themselves just a little closer to the truth. One of the problems was the apparent lack of remorse, and without that spur Fr Smyth continued his role-playing, using whichever of his guises dealt with awkward questions. He would make admissions only when confronted with the truth. A number of people who knew Fr Smyth have described him as a 'loner', someone who appeared to enjoy his own company and who revealed little of his real personality. There is little doubt that this was a deliberate policy perfected by the priest to maintain an air of mystery as to the true nature of his life. Given this attitude it seems certain that those police officers who interviewed him would have found it difficult to make any impact on a man who would volunteer nothing, a man, too, who would have spurned this opportunity to cleanse himself of years of wrongful abuse of children, to unburden himself of guilt for the hurt he had caused. To expect Fr Smyth to open up and tell everything to the police is to make an assumption that there was in the priest a recognition that his deeds were wrong.

The police investigation began in February 1990 after Susan had made her allegations against Fr Smyth to a social worker employed by the Catholic Family Welfare Society in Belfast. I am told that from the outset Fr Smyth made it as difficult as he possibly could for the investigators. Not only did he go on the run for more than two years but he resisted telling the whole truth. His attitude was that if the police did not know the exact nature of his offences, he certainly was not going to tell them. It has been suggested that he would acknowledge the accusations as they were repeated to him. He admitted some but on others he would maintain an aloof pose occasionally mixed with a hint of sarcasm. At times he would not confirm allegations but would not deny them outright either. He would apparently say something along the lines of: 'If that is what you say, then it must be true.' In order to minimise his involvement, Fr Smyth had, like other paedophiles, developed a defence mechanism which meant he would admit to 'tickling' his accusers as if that was all that was meant by their charges. In fact when he owned up to 'tickling' he was admitting a sexual activity, most likely fondling – a classic case of a paedophile using innocent words to describe criminal acts which the perpetrator could not bring himself to admit were in any way wrong.

Abbot Kevin Smith, in a conversation with one of those whom Fr Smyth abused, described the priest as someone who could not admit his guilt. When confronted with allegations and told that the Abbot wanted him to go for treatment he would acquiesce, stating that if that was what the Abbot wanted then he would do it. There was at no stage an admission by Fr Smyth that he needed treatment; he merely indicated that for a quiet life he would go along with the Abbot's wishes. There is no reason to assume that this attitude changed with the police or prison staff as they sought information about criminal acts, or tried to build up a personality profile for the prison records. It is my firm impression, reinforced by a conversation I had with someone who was in Magilligan prison when the priest was sent there, that he simply does not believe he has done any wrong. To the priest, it was acceptable to satisfy his sexual cravings. It has been suggested that he thought one of the young girls he abused by putting his hands into her underwear and touching her genital area, actually liked this behaviour. He was heard to say: 'Yes, she did not bother about it at all.' He claimed that she did not object to his kissing her on the mouth.

Again, these are not untypical of the paedophile's attempts to justify his actions or to diminish his guilt, to make them seem less harmful to individuals than they really are. Of course, time was a major factor since Smyth was facing questions about offences going back more than twenty years. This inevitably created problems in the recall of events so far distant in the past. There is ample evidence that he particularly felt sexually attracted to boys and girls in the eight to eleven age group, 'tickling' them to get some kind of sexual gratification. It is my under-standing that while he would have difficulty admitting that 'tickling' was a criminal offence, he clearly knew the meaning of the word 'paedophile': he understood perfectly well that such an individual was someone sexually attracted to children, even admitting on occasion that he saw himself as a paedophile. This did not prompt him to go that one step further and make a clean breast of the offences he had committed.

By talking to those the priest had abused it was relatively easy for the police to build up a picture of his method of operating, and it is interesting to note that Fr Smyth admitted charges relating to abuses which took place in Church-run institutions. He was able to remember asking unwitting nuns to fetch girls from class at St

Dominic's High School, having used his priestly status to gain access. Similarly, I am given to understand, he did not deny going into Nazareth House to visit Siobhan. Although there were charges relating to the priest's having engaged in digital penetration of some of those he abused I am told he constantly denied this. He has, however, apparently gone on record as having done this 'once with an adult', giving the excuse that he just wanted to see what it felt like.

Staff at Magilligan Prison near Limavady in County Derry had little knowledge of the new face in the sex offenders' wing. But they do have an expertise in the understanding of the mind of the paedophile. They help prepare such people for rehabilitation into society (Fr Smyth will be released in 1996 providing he gets full remission). Magilligan has developed its own three-stage programme to deal with sex offenders: in the first instance it attempts to get the convicted paedophile to look closely at the nature of their offences; secondly, it considers empathy with the victim, and the final part of the programme looks at means of preventing re-offending on release. This system was devised by staff at the jail after they had studied methods employed at a number of other prisons in the United Kingdom including a scheme introduced at a Scottish prison in January 1993, which is being seen by many experts as perhaps offering the best way forward in dealing with the problems of paedophilia.

Peterhead Prison is situated about 30 miles north of Aberdeen. It was once a high security jail housing murderers and dangerously violent inmates; today it retains its top security status but it has become a holding centre for sex offenders – the only one of its kind in the United Kingdom. The Governor, Alec Spencer, has been instrumental in pioneering a programme specially aimed at dealing with the problem of paedophilia. The programme sets out with the knowledge that once released paedophiles will re-offend. As there is no known method of removing from them the desire for sexual relations with children, the intention is to equip them with an intellectually acceptable means of resisting temptation. Prison staff are given special training to conduct the group sessions required to make the programme work and they have the benefit of advice and consultation with psychologists, psychiatrists and social workers. Once suitable volunteers from the prison's paedophile population have been chosen for the programme, they face four crucial stages:

1   The prisoners face up to their responsibilities.

As most tend to deny they have done anything wrong, the aim during group sessions is to make them face up to the fact that they cannot minimise or justify the horrific offences they committed.

2   The abusers look at the victims of their perversion.

The idea is to get them to realise that those they sexually assaulted were not objects for the fulfilment of their lustful desires but people, human beings with names and feelings. Part of this exercise involves writing letters to those molested although the letters are never ever mailed.

3   This stage focuses on what is termed the 'offence cycle'.

The offenders are made to think about their crimes, their fantansies while looking at pornography, their targeting of children and grooming them for the offences. Paedophiles go to considerable trouble to identify children for abuse either within their own family circle or by getting involved in activities with groups of children.

4   Relapse prevention

This section of the programme tries to make the paedophile understand that just because he has thoughts about a child, it does not mean he is offending. They are told that they may think about such things but it does not become an offence until they make something happen. So, before going that far, they should stop.

The Peterhead experiment is in its infancy; the full programme takes over a year and insufficient numbers of offenders have been released as yet. It is still impossible to gauge its success rate but as it is modelled on a system developed in Canada by Professor Bill Marshall, the Canadian conclusions may be relevant. According to Alec Spencer, there is evidence that in Canada the numbers re-offending have been reduced by 30 to 35 per cent.

10

CHASING SHADOWS

1: PRIEST ON THE RUN

I felt cheated that he'd been allowed to run so long. I don't understand why people shielded him when so many people knew what he was like. I think the church shielded him quite a lot. I mean once he was down south he was in a different country where he couldn't be got at and it was only when he came up here to the North . . . that's the only time they could have arrested him.

Bernie, mother of children abused by Fr Smyth.

That Fr Brendan Smyth was flushed out of his hiding place in the Republic and into a Belfast court owes more to the tenacious spirit of Bernie and Seamus than it does to the forces of justice in Dublin or the Catholic Church authorities, who failed in their duty to hand over a self-confessed paedophile. Fr Smyth's decision to place himself outside the jurisdiction and to remain beyond the reach of the RUC for almost three years is perhaps matched by the attitude shown by his employers. In the face of adversity and public humiliation, each adopted a head-in-the-sand attitude in the hope that the paedophile priest's problems would disappear. To the RUC, pursuing Fr Smyth was like chasing shadows, in much the same way as I was to find later when I attempted to get someone from the Catholic Church to admit responsibility for the priest. Chasing the shadows which tumbled out of Fr Smyth's cupboard once his cover was blown has become a way of life for Bernie and Seamus. If people thought this pair could be diverted from their path, and there were those who tried to do so, they were to be deeply disappointed.

From the moment they first learned about Fr Smyth they were determined to get to the truth and to make the priest accountable for his actions. They hoped they would enjoy the support of Fr Smyth's order and the Church. Rejection by the Abbot at their meeting in Armagh in 1989 has only helped to galvanise their anger, channelling it into a sustained effort to find justice for their children.

In this context the significance of their 1989 Armagh meeting with Abbot Smith cannot be overlooked. If the Abbot had not spent so much time extolling the virtues of the paedophile priest and if he had promised Bernie and Seamus some kind of positive action, the whole problem might well have been resolved there and then. Bernie and Seamus would not have been lost to the Catholic faith and in all probability, Fr Smyth's potential for causing widespread damage to the Church and his central role in the collapse of a government might never have happened. As it was, Abbot Smith spurned this opportunity to rid himself, the abbey and the Church of his problem priest. Of course, the simple answer would have been to turn the paedophile over to the law in Northern Ireland but for some reason the Abbot chose not to follow that line of action either. If he reasoned he could keep Fr Smyth away from trouble long enough to allow the horrible mess to disappear it was ill-founded logic. Then there was always the 'transfer' option, moving the problem out of the way. That had worked in the past! However, things were not quite the same this time, even though Fr Smyth had not walked away from another violated child or a household distraught upon seeing through his priestly disguise – this time he had walked out of a police station on £100 bail!

As the police continued to gather evidence, Bernie and Seamus and more importantly their children were dismayed and alarmed to see the man they had reported to the police still walking the streets of West Belfast. They kept up the pressure on the RUC, the Church hierarchy and the Abbot of Kilnacrott in a campaign of letters and telephone calls. As we shall see, their campaign was vital in bringing the priest to trial but there's another reason to be grateful for their efforts to keep the Fr Smyth case moving. It is possible to study the responses they were given at various stages of the ongoing police investigation and make comparisons with the key statements eventually made in 1994 by Cardinal Daly and Abbot Smith. In this way it is possible to put together a picture of how the Catholic Church and the Norbertine Order reacted to events during the RUC investigation which began in 1990 and ended in 1994. To Catholics like Bernie and Seamus the performance of the Church, the order and the Cardinal fell short of what they expected, of what they believed should have been done to ensure that the priest faced up to the hurt and pain he had caused their family. In short, having been brought up in the Catholic faith and having reared their own children in the ways of the faith, Bernie and Seamus found themselves in the uncomfortable position of having to take stock of their Church at a time of family crisis. What makes it even more painful is that their journey of discovery in relation to the Church is not over; it may have begun in 1988, but it continues even today.

One of the first letters written by Bernie and Seamus was sent to Ballyjamesduff in County Cavan. On 4 February 1991 Abbot Smith sent this reply:

I thank you for your good letter recvd. [sic] here today. I understand your concern. However, there is no way I can prevent Fr Brendan Smyth from going to Belfast. He is a man of almost 65 years of age. However, I can assure you that he is attending a professional sexual counsellor twice each month and they will continue for some time. He attends Dr Del Monte in St James Hospital, Dublin. I have monitored the situation several times with him and he assures me that everything is going well. Likewise I talk to Fr Brendan often too. There is nothing more that I can do. We must also pray for him.
With my good wishes,
Yours sincerely,
Kevin A. Smith, O. Praem. Abbot.

Even at this late stage the Abbot appeared to be disinclined to do anything more than offer prayers for the priest and apparently refused to restrict his movements. This power to restrict movement, I'm given to understand, was part of the Abbot's right as Fr Smyth's religious superior. One notices that there is not one word of prayer offered for Bernie's four abused children. Bernie and Seamus regarded this correspondence as little more than an insult to them and their children.

A week later on 11 February, Cardinal Daly responded thus to a letter from Bernie:

(I cannot be sure that this is the correct name, but I hope that the letter will reach your address). There have been complaints about this priest before and once I had to speak to the Superior about him. It would seem that there has been no improvement. I shall speak with the Superior again. I am very sorry for the distress which your family had been experiencing and I hope that the problem can be solved quickly and that you will have no further interference. Asking God to bless you and with all kind wishes,

Yours sincerely,
+Cahal B. Daly.
Archbishop of Armagh.

The Cardinal had no need for concern over the correct name. It was the same name as that given by Susan in 1990 when her complaints about Fr Smyth to a social worker from the Catholic Family Welfare Society led to the police investigation approved of by the Cardinal. But what of his reference to having had 'complaints about this priest before'? This has never been fully explained because he has consistently declined my requests for an interview. Who made these earlier complaints? In the absence of clarification from the Cardinal, I will try in the next chapter to establish the identity of the persons who made these earlier complaints by using existing evidence and deductions therefrom.

To understand Cardinal Daly's position in relation to the Fr Smyth affair more fully it is necessary to know that prior to the vast wave of publicity which followed transmission of *Suffer Little Children*, the Cardinal rejected the opportunity to be interviewed. It was only after the programme had been screened that he offered his thoughts in any detailed manner, mostly to express the Church's regret at the suffering the priest had caused. It was not until 5 December 1994 that he decided to provide the definitive statement setting out his knowledge of the affair and the details of the actions he took in dealing with Fr Smyth. This lengthy statement (nearly 1,400 words) was issued to counter what the Cardinal termed 'the widespread public misunderstanding about my own role relative to the Father Smyth case'. Central to the whole Fr Smyth affair has been the question of when the Cardinal first became aware of the paedophile priest. One must remember that the majority of Fr Smyth's criminal acts took place in the diocese of Down and Connor where the Cardinal served as bishop from October 1982 until December 1990, when he became Archbishop of Armagh. On the issue of his first knowledge, the Cardinal had this to say on 5 December 1994:

On 23 February 1990 a client, accompanied by a parent, visited the offices of the Catholic Family Welfare Society in Belfast. They were interviewed by one of the society's social workers. The client told the social worker about sexual abuses suffered at the hands of Fr Brendan Smyth over a period of years. The social worker offered advice. She obtained the family's permission to inform the RUC and she did, in fact, report the allegations to the police. She also urged the family themselves to inform the RUC. Subsequently the social worker informed the statutory health and social services authorities. The social worker also informed the priest director of the Catholic Family Welfare Society (a priest of the diocese of Down and Connor) who in turn informed my priest-secretary. My secretary immediately informed me. I approved of the steps taken and specifically expressed my approval of the fact that the allegations had been reported to the police.

It is worth establishing exactly what this passage from the Cardinal means in relation to the facts. We know that Susan went to see the social worker about a matter entirely unrelated to Fr Smyth and she went with her father Seamus although, contrary to what the Cardinal states, Seamus says he was not in the room during the interview between Susan and the social worker. However, because of the nature of this other matter, it is clear that the social worker knew the family name. So when the Cardinal talks about the family of this 'client' also being urged to go to the police the family name was known. What is more, in his 1994 statement the Cardinal reveals that after he had approved of the involvement of the police in 1990 and because 'of the gravity of the matters reported to me, I sought a meeting with the Abbot.' Then he states: 'The meeting took place on 12 March 1990. I informed the Abbot about the complaints. I told him that a social worker had seen the client and that the allegations of abuse had been reported to the RUC. The Abbot accepted full responsibility for Fr Smyth and undertook to take prompt and appropriate steps to deal with the matter.' As we all know now, Abbot Smith did not act to expedite the Fr Smyth case: the priest carried on living in the abbey with the full knowledge of the Abbot. From 8 March 1991 onwards, the telephone calls from the RUC persisted, with messages being left for Fr Smyth. The person who answered the telephone and Abbot Smith clearly knew that the police were actively involved in an investigation which, as the Cardinal told the Abbot, had begun on 23 February 1990.

Consider then the statement the Abbot issued on 26 September 1994: 'I was not aware of any desire on the part of the RUC or the Garda Siochana to interview or serve process upon Fr Smyth. I did not know that the extradition of Fr Smyth was sought or contemplated.' In the light of the aforementioned telephone calls it seems strange that he was not aware of the RUC interest. The RUC investigation began with the Cardinal's approval in February 1990 and involved the very family the Abbot had met at an hotel in Armagh during the previous year. In fact, the Abbot's statement refers to this meeting: 'In 1989 I received complaints from a family about Fr Smyth's conduct with their children. Twice thereafter, Cardinal Daly, then Bishop of Down and Conor [sic] communicated with me and requested that I, as Fr Smyth's religious superior, take appropriate steps to deal with Fr Smyth's misconduct. Dr Patrick Walsh, the present Bishop of Down and Conor [sic], also contacted me regarding the same issue. After the 1989 complaint I had arranged for Fr Smyth to attend a clinical psychologist in Dublin regularly and so informed the bishops. I also gave assurances to both bishops that I would deal effectively with Fr Smyth.' So here Abbot Smith says that Cardinal Daly knew about Fr Smyth in 1989 and what's more, that the people making the complaint to the Abbot in 1989 were the same family that became involved with the social worker in 1990, the case on which Cardinal Daly says he was fully briefed and in respect of which he gave his approval for police involvement. It was the same family that wrote to him in February 1991. Yet, in his definitive statement of 5 December 1994, Cardinal Daly does not mention this 1989 complaint of which he was apparently made aware by the Abbot.

When the Cardinal received Bernie's letter in February 1991, he was fully aware that a police investigation had begun into Susan's allegations and in his statement of 5 December 1994 he acknowledges this letter had come from 'the same family'. The Cardinal states that he immediately contacted the Abbot again, emphasising the need for him to take firm action to deal with Fr Smyth. He also reveals that the Abbot wrote to him on 21 February 1991 (ten days after the Cardinal had written to Bernie).

The Cardinal's statement read:

He [the Abbot] told me that Father Brendan Smyth had denied that there had been 'any incident of that nature for a couple of years now', and that Father Smyth 'only goes to Belfast to visit his doctor and otherwise only visits his own family'.

By this time Fr Smyth was under police investigation, as the Cardinal was very much aware, having himself been kept fully informed and having approved of the involvement of the police.

The Cardinal's next paragraph says that at or about this time in 1991 he learned the police investigations were approaching conclusion and court action was anticipated. Indeed by the end of February 1991 the police were ready to interview the priest and the date agreed was 8 March. Detectives watched Fr Smyth leave Grosvenor Road police station at lunchtime that day after three hours of questioning, during which time he made admissions about sexually abusing children, providing sufficient grounds for nine charges to be preferred against him. They warned him there would have to be a preliminary enquiry in a few weeks time and they would need to see him prior to that so he could receive papers relating to the case. Little did they realise they would not again have him as a guest in their interview rooms until 1994. At this stage the police had statements from five witnesses alleging abuse by Fr Smyth and once he had been taken in for interview he was asked to sign a 'voluntary attendance' certificate, required under the Police and Criminal Evidence Act (PACE), to show that he was making himself available for questioning on a voluntary basis at this stage and that he was not under arrest. Fr Smyth signed this form at ten o'clock in the morning.

Throughout the morning he declined all offers of food and when asked if he wanted to wait in the reception area while charge sheets were prepared he chose to remain in the interview room – sensitive perhaps to being seen in his priest's clothing in the reception area of a busy West Belfast police station. Three hours after entering the station, he was charged on nine counts and it is my understanding that in spite of the doubts of some detectives about the wisdom of releasing the priest, police bail was in fact arranged for him with his own surety of £100. So he walked out free to resume his duties as supply chaplain to the Irish army in Monaghan and Cavan. From the moment of his release on bail the priest embarked on what is now viewed as a deliberate policy destined to hamper the advancement of the court case against him – not just by running over the border where he was out of reach of the RUC but also by taking legal steps.

As the police continued to prepare a file on Fr Smyth for consideration by the Director of Public Prosecutions office, the next legal move was to set a date for a preliminary enquiry, a court hearing at which Fr Smyth would be expected to appear to be formally charged. The date chosen for this was 3 April 1991, although it appears this was put back at the request of the priest through his solicitor Denis Moloney who made an approach to a senior member of the RUC. Someone forgot to tell the court and when on 3 April Fr Smyth was called he was not present! During the summer of 1991 papers were in the process of being prepared for service on the priest and on 25 July the Fr Smyth file was returned to police from the DPP's office marked 'Prosecute'. A new date, 16 August, was set for the postponed preliminary enquiry but by now the police were experiencing difficulty in tracking down Fr Smyth.

Months had gone by and all their efforts to speak to the priest had failed. They knew he was based at the abbey at Kilnacrott in County Cavan and so there were regular telephone calls there in an attempt to speak to him of the need to meet so that these papers could be served on him. During these calls to the abbey, messages were left stating the name, rank and telephone number of the RUC officer trying to make contact with Fr Smyth. None of these calls was returned and it was not until 6 December 1991 that by chance a police officer finally got to speak to the priest, simply because Fr Smyth happened to answer the telephone. The priest was quickly appraised of the situation: the RUC needed to see him in the North so he could be served with papers containing the statements of allegation against him and his own statements made during the interview on 8 March. It was explained that once he had been given the papers, a summons would then be issued for his appearance in court where he would be returned for trial to Belfast Crown Court. Fr Smyth told this officer he had no plans to come North at the moment, 'until way next year', as he put it, apparently ignoring the urgency and seriousness of his position at this time.

I've been given to understand that at this stage, the police officer informed the priest if he did not agree to arrange a date for service of the papers in Northern Ireland, the police would have no alternative but to seek his extradition. The officer put it to the priest that he would not want that to happen given the publicity that his being handed over at the border would attract. Fr Smyth simply repeated that he might be up in Northern Ireland some time next year, clearly challenging the authority of the police and making it known that as long as he was outside the jurisdiction he did not feel compelled to comply with the wishes of the RUC. The priest said he would call in at Grosvenor Road station 'some time' but months went by and he did not appear. It was at this point that extradition made its first appearance on the agenda as a very real possibility.

Watching these events very closely from the wings were the abused who made the initial statements to the police: Anthony, Susan, her brothers and sister ... and, of course, Bernie and Seamus. The priest's desire to avoid the RUC was delaying proceedings but as a tactic it was to backfire. It was during this period that police got another breakthrough, making contact with John, who agreed to be interviewed and whose statement provided the RUC with the most serious allegations in the investigation so far. Having made the moves to report the paedophile priest to the police, the abused found the pace of the investigation frustrating and could not understand why Fr Smyth was not being made amenable to the Northern Ireland authorities. It galled them that he was still to be seen walking around streets in their area, regularly visiting homes still on his list and where his paedophile activities were either not known about or had been heard about but not believed.

Time moved on and still Fr Smyth remained out of reach of the police. They asked Fr Smyth's solicitor if he would accept service of the priest's papers but Fr Smyth refused to consent to this. The first steps towards extradition were taken early in 1992 and by August of that year Bernie had once again written to Cardinal Daly reiterating the family's dismay at the lack of progress in making the priest available for prosecution. With the priest firmly entrenched at Kilnacrott Abbey and unwilling to return North to face trial, Bernie had by this stage become concerned that he was being shielded by the Church. Although she does not have a copy of the letter she wrote to the Cardinal, Bernie does remember the sentiment of the communication, that she questioned the Cardinal over what she termed 'a cover-up', expressing the view that she thought the priest was being protected and because he had not been handed over to the police, he was still free to roam the streets of Belfast in his clerical clothing with the obvious risk this entailed for other children.

The Cardinal responded in a letter dated 18 August 1992:

I have just received your letter and I thank you for writing. I am sorry to hear that the trouble continues and I understand your deep concern for your own family and for other children. But when you speak of a 'cover-up' by the Church, I don't think that it is justified. The Church, in the sense of the Bishops, are certainly not 'covering-up' for anyone. The recent TV programme about this question praised the Irish Bishops for being the pioneers in facing up to the problem as far as their priests are concerned. But Father Smyth is not governed by a Bishop but by his own Abbot and only his Abbot can tackle the problem. When you wrote to me before, I was Bishop of Down and Connor and was therefore Bishop of the place when the incidents occurred. I therefore wrote to the Abbot and asked him to meet me. He assured me Father Smyth was then receiving the appropriate treatment and that according to reports he was doing very well under treatment. He said that the treatment was taking place in Belfast and this was why Father Smyth had to visit Belfast for purposes of the treatment. There was nothing more I could do then. Being no longer Bishop of Down and Connor, I do not have the same right to intervene; nevertheless if there is anything I can do I shall certainly do so. I repeat my very sincere sympathy and assure you of my prayers. Please remember me in your prayers. With all kind wishes,

Yours sincerely,
+Cahal Cardinal Daly.
Archbishop of Armagh.

Treatment in Belfast? Cardinal Daly stated he was told by the Abbot that Fr Smyth was making his frequent trips to Belfast to get treatment; yet in his letter to Bernie the Abbot stated clearly that treatment was taking place in Dublin. Where lies the truth? To discover that we must again leap forward in time to a letter of 26 September 1994, when the Abbot set out details of Fr Smyth's programme of treatment going back twenty-six years:

In 1968 we sought treatment for Fr Smyth at Purdys-burn Hospital in Belfast where aversion techniques were used. At that time psychiatrists believed that this was the appropriate treatment for his disorder. In time it became apparent that it was not effective in this case. In 1973 Fr Smyth was again sent for treatment, this time at St Patrick's Hospital in Dublin. In 1974 Fr Smyth was institutionalised for a time at Stroud in Gloucestershire. In 1989 he was referred by the community (Norbertine Order) for further treatment by a Consultant Psychologist in Dublin. Fr Smyth attended him on a regular basis until late last year (1993). From his history you see that we sought expert intervention and treatment for Fr Smyth.

From what the Abbot reveals, it is clear Fr Smyth's treatment in Belfast was confined to a period of unspecified duration around 1968, although the inference is clearly that this treatment concluded prior to his next spell of treatment at St Patrick's Hospital in Dublin. Remember that in his letter to Bernie in February 1991 he stated Fr Smyth was getting treatment at a Dublin hospital where he 'is attending a professional sexual counsellor twice each month and that will continue for some time.' There is absolutely no mention of Belfast. So where was Fr Smyth receiving treatment? Why the apparent contradictions? It hardly inspires confidence that the Church and the order cannot agree on something so basic as to exactly where the priest was receiving treatment – at least, that is the impression given in their statements and correspondence.

As it happens, Bernie's letter to the Cardinal in August 1992 resulted in the Cardinal once again speaking to Abbot Smith at Kilnacrott. By this time, of course, the priest had been evading the police for more than a year, so work in preparing extradition warrants was going on.

Telephone lines into the offices of the detectives investigating the paedophile priest were kept busy, not least
because they were still seeking the priest at Kilnacrott but
because of anxious calls from the families of those abused,
the families who now expected justice and who were
becoming increasingly frustrated whilst the priest remained
at large. They now viewed the Catholic Church as a
protector of a criminal, a sex offender still at large on the
streets of Belfast and whose appearance was very upset-
ting to those individuals who had reported him to the
police. As far as Bernie was concerned she and her
children were being denied justice: 'I felt cheated that he'd
been allowed to run so long. I don't understand why
people shielded him when so many people knew what he
was like. I think the Church shielded him quite a lot. I
mean once he was South he was in a different country
where he couldn't be got at and it was only when he came
up here to the North, that's the only time they could have
arrested him.'

But Fr Brendan Smyth proved as slippery as an eel: even
when he was seen in Belfast and the police were informed,
he still managed to get away. The reason for this was as
much the political climate in West Belfast at the time as
the priest's ability to avoid the detectives he had last seen
at Grosvenor Road police station on 8 March 1991. Normal
policing was not possible in an area of IRA strength: there
had been instances in the past when police officers had
been lured into an ambush by means of a hoax call for help.
The result was that procedures were put in place to safe-
guard officers which had the effect of delaying police
response time. By the time police officers responded to calls

about the priest he had moved on. Mind you, this does not explain how he was able to move so freely backwards and forwards over the border where security checks were conducted on most vehicles making the crossing. When RTE's Joe Duffy managed to get inside Magilligan Prison to see Fr Smyth late in 1994, the priest alleged that the RUC could have apprehended him at border security checkpoints as he drove through in his Northern registered car. Whatever the case, and it could be that the RUC missed him during this time, Fr Smyth simply did not make himself available to the police at Grosvenor Road police station in Belfast for service of the papers relating to the case, as he had apparently promised to do.

As 1992 came to a close, work was proceeding slowly with preparation of the extradition warrants. Extreme care was being taken to ensure no slip-ups of the kind witnessed in the past involving crimes of a more 'political' nature. As it was put to me, every 'i' was dotted and every 't' was crossed by the time the warrants were placed for signing before a Belfast magistrate on 23 April 1993. Within six days they were with gardai in Dublin and a day later, on 30 April 1993, copies were passed on by gardai to the Department of Justice and the Attorney-General's office. The Attorney-General in question, Harry Whelehan, has gone on record as stating he was unaware the Fr Smyth warrants had reached his department until October 1994, when our programme, *Suffer Little Children* reported that the warrants were never executed. This fact was seized upon by a number of TDs, who raised questions in the Dáil.

Confirmation that Mr Whelehan was not aware of the nine RUC warrants came from Matthew Russell, the senior official in his department, who told the Dáil committee of inquiry into the Fr Smyth affair on Wednesday, 21 December 1994:

Mr Whelehan was guilty of no dishonesty whatever. He never knew of the Smyth case because I did not inform him of its existence and he had no other means of learning of its existence.

Mr Russell went to great length to explain his reason for not processing the warrants, placing on record his disdain at rumour and speculation of an outside influence and stating categorically before the committee that he is not a member of Opus Dei and never had been. He went on:

The only contact of any kind which any persons had with me about the case were, firstly the written communication of 30 April 1993, from the gardai, consisting of a covering minute and copies of the warrants and supporting documentation which they had received from the RUC; secondly, the submission dated 31 May 1993, from the Chief State Solicitor's Office raising a number of legal issues about the warrants and their supporting documentation; and thirdly, the four telephone communications from officials in the English Attorney-General's Office, the first on 20 September 1993, and the others on 14 October, 18 November and 6 December. The last of these was to tell me that they had been informed that Father Smyth would be returning voluntarily to Northern Ireland.

Mr Russell cited legal considerations and the burden of work as the reason for the delay in dealing with the case, explaining that during the period the Fr Smyth file was on his desk he gave priority to advisory aspects of six bills and was dealing with twelve other extradition cases, so that his work on the Fr Smyth case was restricted to intervals when he could devote time to it. He told the committee:

> I freely admit that in the Smyth case the judgment has been found to be wrong and I very much regret that.

Back in Belfast, there were others with good reason to regret this lack of action in the Republic, and for one person in particular, Susan, the strain of waiting for Fr Smyth to come to trial proved too much: she attempted suicide in December 1993. This was after she and her parents, Bernie and Seamus, had become increasingly frustrated and depressed by what they saw as the failure of the authorities to send Fr Smyth back to Northern Ireland. There was a desire on their part to try to reintroduce normality to their lives, something they had not been able to enjoy since 1988 when they first learned of Fr Smyth's betrayal. Reporting the priest to the police was only part of what they hoped would be a process to exorcise Fr Smyth from the lives of their children. The constant delays meant the family was still facing what they knew was going to be a traumatic experience, Fr Smyth's court case. As far as they were concerned, Fr Smyth was on the run but yet still appeared to be making visits to

Belfast; members of the family had spotted the priest's car in nearby streets and he had once been seen outside a bank on the Falls Road. The Church authorities were not taking action to have him returned to the North. They viewed this as yet another example of what they saw as the Church caring more for its image than for those abused by Fr Smyth. What Bernie, Seamus and Susan did next was perhaps the most important single factor in finally resolving the problem of the priest on the run.

It was October 1993 when the sheer frustration of waiting for justice finally prompted this determined trio to tackle the problem from a different angle. They began making telephone calls to Cardinal Daly's office in Armagh. Susan's life was in turmoil, not only because of the distress of the abuse by Fr Smyth but also because as the year drew to a close her marriage was facing difficulties and her approach to a local priest for assistance had backfired badly. He suggested nothing which could help her overcome her problems, but simply expressed his regret that she was having them. As it happens this was the same priest who on another occasion had called to see Susan's parents about the possibilities of getting two of their children to become altar boys. Because of the family's experience the priest was shown the door pretty swiftly, although next day Bernie regretted being quite so sharp with him and visited the church to explain the reason for the family's distress. She says he listened to what she had to say and appeared to go pale as she gave the details of the abuses her four children suffered. It is hardly surprising that priest could offer little by way of comfort: he too was soon to be arrested by the RUC on foot of a series of allegations relating to sexual abuse of boys.

It was against this background that Bernie, Seamus and Susan moved to get the support of the head of the Catholic Church in Ireland. According to Susan, Seamus made the first call, a forlorn attempt to do something positive as he watched members of his family crumble emotionally. Susan tried next, then Bernie, but like Seamus they did not get the opportunity to speak to the Cardinal directly. She said that between them they made six unsuccessful attempts to talk to Cardinal Daly. When Susan's story appeared in *The Irish Times* on Wednesday, 19 October 1994, reporter Alison O'Connor contacted the Catholic Church press office to check out whether or not the Cardinal could remember the calls. This is what Ms O'Connor wrote:

> She described failed attempts to contact Cardinal Cahal Daly but the Cardinal has strongly rejected the claims that he refused to take her calls. A spokesman at the Catholic press office said the Cardinal would have arranged a meeting with her if she had telephoned. This is his policy and he is absolutely certain he would have taken the call. The name would have rang [sic] a bell and he would have recognised it.

The family was outraged at this response and their anger was focused on proving the Cardinal's statement to be false.

It did not take Bernie too long to trace the priest who

was the Cardinal's secretary at the time and with the aid of a small tape recorder she contacted him by telephone to see if he could shed any light on the matter. Imagine her relief when he said that of course he remembered the name, and remembered the calls. Now Bernie's anger was directed towards those who issued the Cardinal's denial of Susan, the Catholic press office in Dublin. In the face of demands for a retraction with equal prominence in the paper, the office promised to look into the matter, check the facts with the priest who had been the Cardinal's secretary and if it was as they had just reported it, then a retraction would be forthcoming. The family waited and waited. Finally, on 28 October 1994, a letter appeared in *The Irish Times* under the heading, 'Paedophile Priest'. It was written by the director of the Catholic Church Press and Information Office, Jim Cantwell:

In a report in The Irish Times *of October 18th,* [the article actually appeared on 19 October] *you quoted a spokesman for this office as saying that a 22-year-old woman who had been sexually abused as a child by Father Brendan Smyth had not, as she stated, contacted Cardinal Daly's office by 'phone last autumn. The statement by this office, in response to a query by* The Irish Times, *was made after a telephone enquiry with the Cardinal, who was then in Rome, and subsequently a conversation with his office in Armagh.*

However, a more thorough check by the Cardinal's office has shown that phone calls were, in fact, received in autumn 1993. The Cardinal did not connect these calls with the Norbertine priest, Father Brendan Smyth. This was so because the caller did not give sufficient information to the Cardinal's secretary to enable the Cardinal to identify Father Smyth as the subject of the telephone calls. The lady also identified herself by a married name which the Cardinal had not previously heard.

The Cardinal assures us that had he known who the caller was, he would have returned her call promptly. I would appreciate the opportunity to place on record the fact that the lady in question did contact the Cardinal's office, contrary to what we, in good faith, told The Irish Times. *We, and the Cardinal, are deeply sorry that this genuine misunderstanding has added to the lady's distress and that of her family.*

This can only be considered a weak response. Certainly, it raised more questions than it answered and it left Bernie, Seamus and Susan absolutely furious. What the Cardinal said is that he did not connect these calls in 1993 with Fr Brendan Smyth. They were calls from a family he first became aware of in 1990 when Susan visited the offices of the Catholic Family Welfare Society and told a social worker of the abuses by Fr Smyth, 'the same family', to use the Cardinal's own words from his statement of 5 December 1994, who communicated with him by way of two letters in 1991 and 1992. The Cardinal refers to the fact that Susan used her married name and that he did not recognise it, and gives the assurance that had he recognised it he 'would have returned her call promptly', in keeping with his policy as quoted by the Catholic

Church press office in 19 October's edition of *The Irish Times*. There are two points to be made about this claim. Firstly, when she twice called the Cardinal's office Susan says she made it clear exactly who was calling, that she was the daughter of Bernie (who had written twice to the Cardinal and received two replies) and Seamus (who had also been calling the Cardinal's office prior to Susan's calls), and that further, during one of Susan's calls she became so angry that her father took the telephone from her to apologise to the Cardinal's secretary; so the name of the family was clearly identified with that of the family who in 1990 had the Cardinal's approval to go to the police. Secondly, though Susan and her complaint were known to the Cardinal in 1990 she did not receive a call from him; in fact, to this day he has not made contact with either Susan or with any member of her family, policy or no policy.

One other question is provoked by Jim Cantwell's explanation in *The Irish Times*, and it is this: if the Cardinal 'did not connect these calls with the Norbertine priest, Father Brendan Smyth', then which paedophile priest did he think the caller was complaining about? Are there so many complaints about paedophile priests going to the Cardinal's office that he has difficulty in recalling which caller is complaining about which priest? This is not really an acceptable excuse, says Seamus, adding: 'We know the Cardinal's office knew exactly who we were when we called and they knew Susan was our daughter. Really it is not good enough and as far as we are concerned the Cardinal has done nothing to deserve our support. I think the Catholic Church in Ireland lives in a time warp, put there by its leadership. We don't want a television leader, we want a leader who deals with everyday life in the Catholic religion and we believe the Catholic religion should not be treated like a political party. We could not meet with the Cardinal to discuss this very important issue because he is busy with other matters. But had we been able to meet him and got a satisfactory explanation, or had we got satisfaction from the Abbot, this matter might not have reached the heights it has reached today.'

After these skirmishes with the Cardinal's office, Bernie, Seamus and Susan faced an unhappy Christmas of 1993 feeling totally estranged from their Church and doubtful that they would ever witness justice. It was at this point that Seamus made yet another call to the Cardinal's residence to explain that his daughter's depression over the Fr Smyth affair had driven her to attempt suicide. Again, according to Seamus, the Cardinal was not available but his office recommended he call the Down and Connor diocese as this was really a matter for Bishop Patrick Walsh. Seamus and Bernie did seek help from their own diocese and although they did not realise it at the time, this was the beginning of the end of their nightmare. They did not succeed in making contact with Bishop Walsh or with the auxiliary Bishop Anthony Farquhar but during one of the calls to the bishop's office in North Belfast someone suggested they contact Monsignor Colm McCaughan. For the first time they found someone in the Church who expressed genuine dismay at their story. 'Monsignor McCaughan gave us hope,' said Seamus. 'He seemed sincere in his expression of regret and astounded when we told him the story of Fr Smyth, especially when we informed him the priest was on the run, that warrants had been issued and that he was still being seen in Andersonstown – and of course he realised immediately the risk to other children. We finally felt someone was going to do something about Smyth.'

Suddenly, from staring adversity in the face during November and at the beginning of December, 1993, Bernie, Seamus, Susan and the rest of their family were facing Christmas with renewed hope that the nightmare journey to a Belfast courtroom was finally nearing an end. Aside from Susan's recovery in hospital, there was real Christmas cheer when Monsignor McCaughan telephoned to say the priest would be returning to Belfast in the New Year. As Seamus put it, 'We had a number of conversations with Monsignor McCaughan during the month of December and then he called to say they had looked into things and because the priest had made verbal admissions and was now a fugitive from justice, the Church had given him a choice, either go up or face being handed over. The monsignor said the Church would not want to harbour a fugitive from justice.'

RUC detectives have since acknowledged that a breakthrough in the deadlock over the extradition request for Fr Smyth was undoubtedly hastened by the efforts of Bernie and Seamus. Kilnacrott Abbey was finally giving up one of its community for trial in a Northern Ireland court on serious child sex abuse allegations. Having ignored Bernie and Seamus for nearly three years, Abbot Kevin Smith responded to the decision of his priest to return North voluntarily by authorising Fr Bernard Marshall to contact the family as Christmas 1993 approached. Bernie and Seamus had tried to get Abbot Smith's help in 1989 when they met him at the hotel in Armagh. Nothing of substance had emerged from this meeting. The RUC had commenced their investigation in February 1990. At the time of the phone call from Fr Marshall the prosecution had been frustrated by Fr Smyth's unavailability, while he was living in Kilnacrott Abbey under the jurisdiction and authority of Abbot Smith. The call from Fr Marshall, during which it was emphasised that Fr Smyth had many positive traits, served only to compound the family's anger. The English Attorney-General's office telephoned the Dublin Attorney-General's office on 6 December 1993 to inform the senior official who had been dealing with the application for Fr Smyth's extradition that since the priest would voluntarily be going back North after Christmas, the warrants should be returned.

The failure of the Irish government to deliver Fr Smyth on foot of the RUC warrants had one important knock-on effect which greatly pleased a number of the abused living in the North. Had the Republic extradited the priest on the nine charges mentioned in the warrants he could be tried only for those offences once he was returned. But because Fr Smyth gave himself up on 21 January 1994, the police were in a position to investigate all the charges that might arise from further allegations against him. And as we now know, there were many, many more.

11

CHASING SHADOWS

2: CHURCH ON THE RUN

A number of priests, writing in the current issue of The
Furrow, *have strongly criticised the Church authorities
on a range of issues, from the handling of the
paedophile priest scandal to the appointment of
conservative bishops without adequate consultation. Fr
Enda McDonagh, professor of moral theology at
Maynooth, describes a common theme: 'A sense of
darkness, of winter darkness, of the darkness of death
has surrounded recent revelations. In Ireland it is said
the old Church is dying.' In the Brendan Smyth case,
the Church authorities ' . . . seemed to some to be
grossly negligent in not following through on early
complaints. Invoking the niceties of ecclesiastical
jurisdiction, however valuable in other contexts, was
considered inadequate to the moral demands of
repeated complaints. Excuses based on ignorance of
the serious consequences for the victims appeared*

too self-serving. The admission of mistakes and the promise of safeguards for the future sounded weak to the genuinely dismayed Catholics and sympathetic others, as well as to those who might be secretly or openly delighted at the embarrassment of the Church.

Andy Pollak, Religious Affairs Correspondent, The Irish Times *(9 January 1995)*

Breaking down the wall of silence carefully erected by the Norbertine Order to protect one of their flock was a task which took more than five months. There is no doubt that the manner in which Abbot Smith chose to deal with Fr Smyth during his twenty-five years as Abbot (and in particular failing to alert the Church authorities in places where Fr Smyth was occasionally placed of his proclivities towards children) meant that the priest was afforded the opportunity to abuse when it should have been long since denied him. The situation was compounded by the lack of information from the Catholic Church press office and Cardinal Cahal Daly. Between them I was left chasing shadows as the Church and the order, sensing a major scandal, allowed senior clerics to ignore the issue of accountability. When the truth eventually emerged it was clear that here was knowledge of Fr Smyth's paedophilia going back almost five decades. The most damning statement of all came from the pen of the Abbot – at least it was he who signed the paper which suggested that Church policy was the removing of problem or paedophile priests from the area where a complaint had been made to a new diocese. But that admission came after months of his dodging my questions. The trail began on Saturday, 9 April 1994, with that first telephone conversation with Abbot Smith and continued with a short letter dated 11 April requesting an interview.

For a quarter of a century Abbot Smith was Fr Smyth's religious superior, the man most likely to be aware of Fr Smyth's unnatural sexual interest in children. Yet rather than hand him over to the forces of justice, for the most part he simply kept moving the priest around. This was in line with Church policy at the time: frequent reassignment of offenders in an effort to keep them from forming attachments to families and children.

Kevin Smith was born in Mountnugent, County Cavan on 24 November 1929 and joined the Norbertine Order a little over two months before his twentieth birthday in 1949. Over the years he had occupied a number of key positions, not least of which was president of St Norbert's College, a secondary school within the abbey grounds which took boarders and which was opened by 1960.

When he took charge of the abbey in 1969, Abbot Smith inherited Fr Brendan Smyth, and by that time there was evidence of the priest's paedophilia. Yet in April 1994 the Abbot was not yet ready to spell out the exact extent of the order's knowledge of Fr Smyth's sexual attraction to children. Admittedly at the time Fr Smyth had not yet come to trial. As the police gathered more evidence from new witnesses the date for the hearing kept being pushed back from what had originally been anticipated as a March appearance. Finally, it looked as though 29 April 1994 would be the date for hearing the case against Fr Smyth, although as things turned out it was to be the briefest of hearings. In court that morning the witnesses against the priest listened from the public gallery as the barrister for the defence explained that Fr Smyth had been taken very ill during a visit to England and was suffering from a heart complaint which had left him hospitalised. That morning a message had been faxed over from a hospital in Gloucestershire stating that Fr Smyth would be confined for a time and would not be fit to travel back to Ireland for some months. So for Bernie, Seamus, their children and the others in court that day who had been abused by Fr Smyth, it looked as though justice was once again facing another delay. Given that the police investigation had begun in 1990 and that they had first interviewed the priest in March 1991, it seemed by April 1994 that the processing of Fr Smyth through the court system was proving an almost impossible task.

By the time Bernie and her family had travelled the short distance from Crumlin Road courthouse to their home in West Belfast, they were all seething with anger as the prospect of the court action continued to hang over their heads. The family could not hope to find peace until the legal moves against the man who had caused them all such pain would be ended.

The adjournment of Fr Smyth's case in Belfast produced a rapid response from Kilnacrott. Within thirteen days of the adjournment there finally arrived a written acknowledgement of my request for an interview delivered to them a month earlier. Dated 12 May, it read:

I acknowledge receipt of your letter of 11 April regarding a member of the Norbertine Order, Fr John Gerald Smyth. As you are aware, charges

*against Fr Smyth were scheduled to be heard at court
in Belfast on Friday, April 29. I understand that the
prosecution of these charges has now been adjourned until next September. Accordingly, I believe it
would be inappropriate to consider your request for
an interview at the moment.*

I remain,

Yours sincerely,

Rev. Gerard Cusack,

O. Praem. Sub-Prior

Our plan to broadcast a detailed account of the life and
times of Fr Brendan Smyth was, naturally, dependent upon
the charges against him being processed through the court
system. We could not transmit before he had been dealt
with in court one way or another; had the court case gone
ahead on 29 April as planned we would have been ready
to run our programme. What would have been missing was
a contribution from the Norbertine Order or the Catholic
Church, as representatives of both were refusing our
invitations to appear before the cameras. With the
postponement of the court proceedings we decided to take
an unusual step: we would send a letter to Abbot Smith
listing in detail the questions arising from the evidence
of individuals Fr Smyth had abused. I say it was unusual
because by taking this course of action we were giving
those who clearly had some difficulty defending their
actions access to the information we had gathered. But it
was our view that we were duty-bound, in the public
interest, to transmit the material we had collected. More
particularly it was in the interests of those who wanted

the Church and the order to be accountable publicly for the activities of Fr Smyth. Their testimony was going to be the focus of the programme, whether or not the Church or the order addressed the issue and made an appearance.

The other reason for forwarding a detailed outline of our programme was to make sure the Church and the order knew we were serious in our intention of transmitting this story, that no matter when the court proceedings were resolved, we were in a position to broadcast at the earliest opportunity and would not necessarily consider ourselves restricted to the normal *Counterpoint* slot on a Thursday night. In any event, on 20 May the following letter was sent to Abbot Smith:

I write regarding a letter from the Rev. Gerard Cusack (dated May 12) in response to my request for an interview about Fr John Gerald Smyth, a member of the Norbertine Order. Whilst I appreciate that Fr Smyth did not appear in court on Friday, April 29, and whilst I also appreciate the difficulty this places you in regarding an interview for transmission after his case has been dealt with in court, I do feel an obligation to make you aware of certain information we have uncovered during our inquiries into the case.

I do this in order to assure that I have made every effort to ascertain from you, and the Catholic Church Press and Information Office in Dublin, answers to questions regarding the way in which the Church has dealt with Fr Smyth's problems as a paedophile during the past 30 years or so. In the interests of fair play, natural justice and public interest, I must be seen to make every effort to provide a platform which accommodates both sides to the story. So it is for this reason I now set out a series of crucial questions which I, and members of the Catholic Church who have assisted my inquiries, are keen to have answered.

It is also worth pointing out that, as I understand, Fr Smyth has admitted most charges levied against him. Once Fr Smyth's case has been prosecuted through the court system, it would be our intention to transmit a detailed report about his life and times as a member of the Norbertine Order. You should know that we are well advanced in our filming for this programme in order that we will be ready to transmit at the earliest possible opening in the UTV schedule following the conclusion of Fr Smyth's case. I want to be sure you have been offered every possible opportunity to comment on matters the film report will raise and so now I propose to outline a number of areas where important questions are to be raised in relation to the employment of Fr Smyth by the Norbertine Order.

Obviously, it would be pertinent to establish when you first became aware of problems relating to Fr Smyth? Individuals we have interviewed claim complaints were made many years ago.

One of the first matters relates to a complaint made to the principal of a school in West Belfast in 1971. The principal was Sister Virgilius and the school was St Dominic's. The sister was made aware of a problem which arose in the school when the daughter of a childhood friend of Fr Smyth complained

*of his behaviour. Sister Virgilius telephoned the girl's
father that day to say Fr Smyth had been told not to
return to the school and that if he, the girl's father,
would not insist on taking the matter further the
Church would deal with it immediately. He agreed to
this course of action, but banned Fr Smyth from ever
returning to his home.*

*What did the Church do about this complaint? Was
it noted on Fr Smyth's personnel file? Were such files
kept? Was Fr Smyth authorised by his Order to travel
to Belfast and to visit St Dominic's and ask for young
pupils to be brought to him in the privacy of a room
provided by the school? Did he have any pastoral role
in Belfast? And why is it that ten years later, he was
back in the same school getting the same access to
pupils? We have interviewed someone who in 1981* [In
fact I later learned that this dating of Susan's
experience was incorrect: Author] *says she was
sexually assaulted by Fr Smyth at St Dominic's.*

*Why was Fr Smyth in the United States? Was he
sent there in a pastoral capacity? Did Abbot Smith
inform Bishop O'Driscoll in the Diocese of Fargo,
North Dakota, about any recorded complaints
concerning Fr Smyth? Again, what did Fr Smyth's
personnel file show at the time of his move to North
Dakota? Why did Fr Smyth return from America
when he did? Were you made aware of difficulties
which had arisen in North Dakota? Was there any
mention of these in the personnel records kept of his
period of employment in the United States? How
much did Fr Smyth earn? He paid a substantial sum*

of money over a two-year period to a young man in the United States to cover the cost of counselling as a result of the problems created by Fr Smyth's sexual advances. When did you become aware of this financial arrangement? Was it approved by you as his Abbot? Did the Order in any way assist with the financial payments to the American? What action did the Order or the Church take when made aware of this arrangement?

I understand Fr Smyth was at some stage sent by the order, or the Church, for treatment. Where did this treatment take place? How often has Fr Smyth been sent on courses of treatment? And when did these take place? After learning of Fr Smyth's problems, what actions did you as his Abbot take to remove him from areas of risk? Since returning from the United States where has Fr Smyth been placed to work? And where was Fr Smyth last placed to work by the Order? Why did it take a year for Fr Smyth to give himself up to the RUC for questioning about complaints made by Catholic worshippers in Belfast? Why did the RUC have to issue extradition warrants? Why did Fr Smyth ignore these warrants for more than a year? During the period the warrants were in place with gardai in the Republic, how often did Fr Smyth travel North of the border? Where did he go? Was it on official Church or Order business and if so what was the nature of this business? Why has a Fr Marshall of the Norbertine Order been telephoning the families of children who allege they were sexually abused by Fr Smyth? What was the purpose of these calls? On whose orders were they made? What help - financial or otherwise - has been offered to the families of children who made allegations against Fr Smyth?

These then are some of the key questions we would like you and the Church to address. I have sent a copy of this letter to Mr Jim Cantwell in the Catholic Press and Information Office. As stated earlier, I have an understanding for the reluctance of you as head of the Norbertine Order to wish to delay addressing these questions, questions which individuals we have interviewed ask for themselves, but I trust you will now be prepared to reconsider your position so that our programme is properly balanced with everyone involved having been offered a chance to have their say. Incidentally, did you ask Fr Smyth if he would be prepared to do an interview with us - one which would not be transmitted until his case has been concluded? We would welcome the opportunity to allow Fr Smyth to have his say. Perhaps you could let me know of his answer.

Yours faithfully,
Chris Moore.
Reporter/Producer, Counterpoint.

This letter is produced in full so there can be no misunderstanding of our position in relation to the seriousness of the allegations being made, not by us, but by members of the Catholic Church. On the day it was written we made another important decision because of the negative response to my requests for interview both to the Catholic press office and the Abbot. It was on this date that I began sending copies of all correspondence directly to Cardinal Daly so that he too would be fully informed at every stage in the development of the story of our position. The response from the abbey was a postcard from the Abbot stating:

A Chara,
I thank you for your letter and encls. of May 20. I have sent them on to our lawyers.

Naturally my telephone calls to both the Catholic Church press office and to the abbey continued. But May became June and suddenly Fr Smyth was scheduled to appear in court on the tenth of the month, a Friday.

This was the day that the footage of Fr Smyth was shot as he walked into Crumlin Road courthouse alongside his solicitor Denis Moloney. He stood in the dock inside listening to seventeen separate charges of indecent assault being read out to him by the clerk, pleading guilty to each. I watched closely from the press gallery as the charges were put to the priest. The fixed expression never left his face even as he watched some of the young women he had abused in childhood break down in tears. The case was adjourned for a week with Fr Smyth being taken into custody for his first night in a prison cell since his first encounter with the police more than three years earlier. A week later I was sunning myself in Crete when the career of the paedophile priest resulted in a four-year jail sentence. *Counterpoint* was off the air and there may have been those who thought the opportunity for a television programme had been missed. It had not; we had decided early in June that even if the priest's case were dealt with we would wait until the autumn to transmit our story.

Back from Crete I waited to discover if the sentencing of Fr Smyth would produce a new attitude at Kilnacrott, Dublin or Armagh. We had now reached July and there was still no response. We continued working towards a transmission date in September or early October when we resumed broadcasting. I even visited the abbey unannounced in the hope of getting an opportunity to speak to the Abbot, but to no avail. In Belfast life was going on as normal although as summer 1994 approached there was much speculation that we would soon be witnessing historic moments as the political process moved towards peace, or at least a ceasefire. In the run-up to the summer break in transmission, *Counterpoint* was busy reflecting the reality of the hopes for peace. In mid-July I took a couple of days off, accepting an invitation from a friend to spend a bit of time at his home in Donegal. When I returned on 14 July it was back to the telephone to pursue the Church authorities once more for answers to my questions. After weeks of unsuccessful attempts to get hold of Abbot Smith this was to prove my lucky day: I was able to speak to him directly in rather the same way as the police officer who happened to get Brendan Smyth: the Abbot picked up the receiver. For the next fifteen minutes of this bright sunny July morning, I had one of the most amazing conversations ever. In the midst of what was clearly a crisis which was not going to go away of its own volition or be dispelled by the powers of persuasion the Abbot talked to me as he might have addressed a schoolboy. Throughout the duration of the call it was as though he was patting me on the head to get me out of his way. His arrogance was staggering, given the enormity of what was about to be revealed:

Author: Hello, Kilnacrott Abbey? Is that Abbot Smith? How are you doing, it's Chris Moore here from . . .

Abbot: Chris Moore, I've been trying to get you, but then I couldn't, you were out, I suppose that was the . . . that was a bad day I suppose.

Author: Oh, aye . . . 'em, so, Abbot, are we in a position where we might be able to meet up and have a chat?

Abbot: About what?

Author: About Fr Smyth.

Abbot: Oh, well that's . . . with our solicitors now. OK? So when they give the OK that will be, have to pass it by them first, you know. OK? When that's, we don't know. We haven't been in touch with him since the courts, so things are kinda . . . at the moment anyway, you know, and we've a death in the community so there's no time for it anyhow.

Author: Right, we're going on air and I think I made it clear in the letter that we're probably going to go on air on the first . . .

Abbot: Sorry?

Author: We're going to be broadcasting our programme on Fr Smyth in September.

Abbot: OK. Right, OK.

Author: And . . . em . . . are you going to be available for interview at some point after you've con . . .

Abbot: That will be dependent on our solicitors, there's other things to come up and we're not going to leave our back open I can tell you that anyway. There's a lot of things to be considered before that.

Author: You were aware of the list of questions I wanted to have...

Abbot: I think those were answered by our solicitors...

Author: I haven't had any answer...

Abbot: Pardon, I thought an answer was sent out to you now.

Author: I have received absolutely nothing by the way of an answer.

Abbot: OK. Yeah, OK. I understood there were answers sent to you now, but maybe you didn't get them...

Author: One simple thing that's really confusing me, I mean where did Fr Smyth acquire twenty thousand dollars to send over to the United States?

Abbot: Well, you know, I, we knew nothing about that so that's another matter altogether, certainly didn't get it from us that's for sure, we weren't aware of that at all. OK. so... that, that thing we weren't aware of at all...

Author: What about...

Abbot: ... through either.

Author: What about previous complaints against Fr Smyth?

Abbot: That wouldn't... that I would presume would have been part of the whole thing whenever it does come off. Eh, I would presume it would be part of the whole thing, wouldn't it?

Author: Yeah, but I mean, there were...

Abbot: Pardon?

Author: ... other complaints against him...

Abbot: Sorry?

Author: You were aware of other complaints ...

Abbot: Sorry?

Author: You were aware of other complaints against him because that's why he was getting treatment, wasn't it?

Abbot: Sorry?

Author: You were aware of other complaints against him because that's why he was being sent for treatment?

Abbot: That, that would be part of what would come up with that.

Author: Can you tell me why was he sent to Cork then, as a, in the last couple of years as a chaplain to an orphanage?

Abbot: He wasn't sent to Cork as a chaplain in an orphanage any time, no way, that's completely untrue.

Author: Oh, but he was still in a position where he was able to have contact with children?

Abbot: Well, you know that's a different matter altogether ...

Author: Yeah, but why was he doing that if there had been complaints about him?

Abbot: Can you, can you 'eh, can can you – is it possible, can you? No you're in a job OK up there, wherever you've a boss, OK does the boss decide where you go out every minute of the day ...

Author: Of course not, no ...

Abbot: No, well there you are, that's your answer.

Author: No, it's not really.

Abbot: Well, it's part of it now Chris ... be ... be

Author: Oh, sure I understand that, Abbot, sure ...

Abbot: Wait, wait now. Come off it now ... use your, hold on, hold on, let me talk ... you talk ... use your logic, use your logic ... use your own logic.

Author: Yes I'm using that, I'm trying to use that ...

Abbot: Well, you're not, you haven't been. Use your logic; don't be hysterical now.

Author: Well, OK. Right, I understand what you are saying ...

Abbot: You have, you have to be logical about it and reasonable. OK?

Author: Yes, I, I..

Abbot: And you can't be asking; you can't be getting, trying to ask impossible questions and get impossible answers. OK?

Author: OK. All right ...

Abbot: And you needn't ...

Author: Look, I accept what you say, right?

Abbot: You're not. Let me finish. You're dealing with an individual who's over twenty-one, who's over twenty-one, who is his own man, who has his own mind as you have, as I have.

Author: Right ...

Abbot: ... and unless he's restricted ... now about that because of a court sentence ... OK? Otherwise there's not, you know it's almost impossible, as you know yourself, as you can restrict where you go what you do, by your bosses up there. Otherwise you'd be kicking up, you'd be taking civil rights away.

Author: I understand that ...

Abbot: There you are well, that, that's your answer.

Author: But what I don't understand, Abbot, OK, and I'm using the same logic because I do understand what you are saying because there are things in my life that my boss doesn't know about.

Abbot: Sure that's right.

Author: But if there had been certain complaints about certain aspects of what I was doing ...

Abbot: Yeah ...

Author: ... to my boss, then I would have thought that my boss would take a particularly careful note 'eh ... be perhaps a little more diligent about what exactly I'm doing.

Abbot: Yeah.

Author: ... And because of the complaints he would have a right to look into my private life a bit more, or what is termed my free time or my down time, but what I'm asking you simply ...

Abbot: Well, now I'll ask you another question.

Author: Right.

Abbot: Having done all that you've said that could be done, and should be done, what, at the end of the day could he do if you want to go to England, Ireland, America and all the rest, he can't stop you unless you end up in jail, isn't that right?

Author: That's right ...

Abbot: Well then that's the logic for you now ... you want to think of that angle as well ....

Author: Sure, I, I ...

Abbot: You see, it's easy, it's easy for people like you to talk when you are just investigating things and trying to find answers. It's easy ... that's the easy part of it but you're always dealing with people who are their own people and you can't take their civil rights away.

Author: But surely Abbot, I mean he would not have been able to go to America with ... to perform in a pastoral role without that having been arranged with the bishop in America and your good self?

Abbot: That's a completely different question altogether.

Author: Well, it's not really ... you've tried to suggest ...

Abbot: Well, it is ...

Author: ... a moment ago that he's free to go to America ...

Abbot: You're dropping now from one to the other OK?, and so aren't you ... if you're free to go, well unless your passport was, was withdrawn ...

Author: Yes, yes.

Abbot: Well, there you are.

Author: Yes, but ... but ... .in a way, yes I agree with you, that's perfectly true, but what I'm saying to you: you're trying to suggest that he's free to go to America any time he wanted to ...

Abbot: If his passport's not withdrawn ...

Author: Yes, but the question is why was he ... I mean any arrangement to get him to America to work in a pastoral sense with the Church as a ... as a parish priest would have to be done through you, would it not?

Abbot: Not necessarily, no ...

Author: Oh, so he can just go and be a parish priest

anywhere he wants . . .

Abbot: Now, I didn't say that . . .

Author: So how did he, who arranged it for him in America?

Abbot: Well, that's another question . . . .

Author: Yes, and have you an answer or haven't you got an answer?

Abbot: I have an answer, yeah of course I have an answer.

[Pause for several seconds]

Author: Well, could you tell me what the answer is?

Abbot: But I'm not giving you the answer . . .

Author: Why?

Abbot: Because I don't want to, that's my privilege to keep the answer to myself as it is your privilege if I don't ask you questions you don't answer . . . that's your privilege. We're . . . we're free human beings . . .

Author: Sure, sure . . .

Abbot: Well there you are . . . free as the lark in the air.

[Author laughs.]

Abbot: OK? Thank you anyway, we'll be back to you when, when we're clear of the solicitors anyway. OK?

Author: Well, tell me, Abbot. Do you think there will come a time when you and I will do an interview?

Abbot: I could not say that at this time . . .

Author: . . . because there's a very strong suggestion from the press office through Jim Cantwell in the press office in a letter he sent the other day that you wouldn't be talking to me.

Abbot: I didn't, well, I don't know what you got . . .

Author: I'll read it to you if you want, I'll let you hear ...

Abbot: No ... no ...

Author: ... what exactly it says ...

Abbot: No, that will be arranged if I have ... it will go to our solicitors and when everything and when the whole thing is cleared up, a lot of issues has to be cleared up before that happens, I can tell you that.

Author: Well, here's what this says: 'It is my understanding that while the Norbertine Community will be responding to your letter of May 20 ...

Abbot: Yeah ...

Author: ... .now that the criminal case against Fr Smyth has been disposed of in court they will not be offering a spokesman for interview on your forthcoming programme. How did he know that you weren't going to speak to me ... ?

Abbot: Because we do everything through the press office, that's part of our ... of the solicitor's idea, plan. They're in charge of it and whatever they say we will do, they'll look after it ... our interests and our rights as well ... OK?

Author: But I've just asked you if you're going to talk to me and you said you had to wait and see.

Abbot: That's right, yeah, that's right, yeah ...

Author: That's a very confusing interview, this chat because ... there appears to ...

Abbot: Chris, because you are making it confusing ...

Author: I'm not ...

Abbot: You won't listen properly ...

Author: I am listening ...

Abbot: You're not ...

Author: I'm waiting ...

Abbot: You're not ...

Author: I'm waiting for you to give me one explanation ...

Abbot: You're not ...

Author: ... about a man who has been running around for thirty years abusing ... children ...

Abbot: ... You don't ...

Author: ... and I haven't yet had an explanation to anything.

Abbot: Don't think ... nobody has to give an explanation to you, remember that.

Author: Of course not ... and nobody's giving an explanation to the members of the Church that he's abused and offended ...

Abbot: No, that ... maybe there has been one given, you don't know ...

Author: I do know ...

Abbot: Do you know everything?

Author: Well, all I know is ...

Abbot: Wait now, wait now ... do you know everything?

Author: Well, that's a stupid question now, do I know everything? Of course I don't know everything ...

Abbot: It's not, it's not, well then that's fine.

Author: Well then, let me tell you the people who are most offended, the people who have been hurt by Fr Smyth in what has happened and have been hurt by the Church, are the people who are yet waiting for an explanation from the Church, I can tell you that ...

Abbot: How . . . .

Author: The people who took Fr Smyth to court, let's put it that way, the people who took him to court, have they been offered any explanation? No.

Abbot: It's you that's saying that now . . .

Author: I am saying it because I'm, I'm . . . I'm in touch with the people. You . . . you, you seem to think I'm working in ignorance here . . . ..

Abbot: Ye . . . no, I didn't say that; you said that.

Author: [slight laugh] . . . No, you haven't said anything really.

Abbot: No, no, no I haven't really, that's true . . .

Author: Because you are obviously very embarrassed by the whole situation – that's the truth of it.

Abbot: You say that too . . .

Author: I am saying that, yes.

Abbot: Well, that's . . . if that's your opinion I've no right to question it as you know . . . 'cause again, 'cause again . . .

Author: I've been courteous enough to give you three pages, two pages of very detailed questions and not one has been answered yet . . .

Abbot: I'm under . . . I'm under no obligation to answer them by the way . . .

Author: Of course not. No, you're not . . .

Abbot: Not in your forum . . .

Author: Well who are you answerable to, Abbot?

Abbot: Pardon, that's that's my business not yours.

Author: But do you . . . who . . .

Abbot: Thank you very much. OK? Thank you now.

Author: What's your relationship with the Cardinal?

Abbot: Thank you very much, Chris. Goodbye, God
bless you; thank you.
[Abbot hangs up at this stage.]

On the basis of this conversation, interviewing Abbot
Smith would appear to involve the same difficulties as
those faced by the police when questioning Fr Smyth;
rambling answers appear to be a common response.

Throughout the period I was preparing this report for
UTV I was receiving absolutely no assistance from anyone
officially connected with the Church and had to rely on
the information unearthed by the abused and their
families. In May one family told me about Fr Smyth's being
sent to Cork as chaplain to an orphanage. This was after
the police had begun their investigation in Belfast and after
he had been interviewed and charged by the RUC on 8 March
1991. Now believing the story to be true, the families were
disgusted. As they saw it, Fr Smyth's crimes were being
covered up and he was being moved out of the way in the
hope that the Belfast investigation would flounder and die.
Late in the summer I went to Cork for a few days with
Counterpoint editor Tony Curry to track down the priest but
we could find no trace of an orphanage, let alone find Fr
Smyth working in one. The Abbot said such a suggestion
was 'completely untrue' and, of course, he was absolutely
correct. The significant thing is not the truthfulness of the
Abbot's response but in what he declined to say, and I view
that as further evidence of his attempts to help a cover-up
for the paedophile priest. Abbot Smith knew when answering
my question that he had given references for Fr Smyth to
be assigned as locum chaplain to a hospital in Tralee on a

number of occasions between August 1990 and September 1993. He also knew that he assigned the priest as locum chaplain to the Mercy Hospital in Cork between 20 September and 19 December 1993. In both hospitals Fr Smyth had access to the children's wards and he performed these duties after being interviewed and charged by the police, and at a time when he was a fugitive from justice with extradition warrants gathering dust in the Attorney-General's office in Dublin. Mercifully, the health authorities who investigated Fr Smyth's periods of duty at the two hospitals found no evidence that he had offended.

The Abbot's day of reckoning was 26 September 1994 and it has since been regarded as the day he did serious damage to the Catholic Church in Ireland with the extent of his admissions about the way Fr Smyth's paedophilia was dealt with over a period of five decades. The three-page letter from the Abbot was dynamite, vindicating the view of the abused and their families that Fr Smyth's life as a child molester had been the subject of a cover-up by his order. A draft of the letter was sent by fax to UTV that day:

Dear Mr Moore,

I refer to your letters, visits and telephone calls to the monastery over the past four months. I have given much thought to your letter of May 20. In an effort to respond to your questions I have reviewed Fr Smyth's history, conferred with the members of our community and sought the advice of professional people who have studied paedophilia.

As Fr Smyth's religious superior at Holy Trinity Abbey since 1969, I acknowledge that I have made many errors in dealing with his wrongdoing. As a community we have also erred and failed in our pastoral response to those who have suffered. At the time of Fr Smyth's conviction we publicly apologised for the hurt caused to so many people. I now again say to those who have suffered that we are heartily sorry.

It is now clear that Fr Smyth should never have had access to children. When he comes out of jail, we as a community are determined to ensure that Fr Smyth has available to him such treatment as is advised. In addition, we are especially alert to the need to do all in our power to ensure he has no further access to children.

Fr Smyth has been a member of the Norbertine Community since 1945. Notwithstanding the absence of records I believe that his problem with children surfaced early in his religious life. In those years frequent reassignment was often the way church authorities handled priest paedophiles and other problem priests. Fr Smyth was reassigned every few years or so in an effort to keep him from forming attachments to families and their children. We now see how inadequate this approach actually was.

In 1968 we sought treatment for Fr Smyth at Purdysburn Hospital in Belfast where aversion techniques were used. At that time psychiatrists believed that this was the appropriate treatment for his disorder. In time it became apparent that it was not effective in this case. In 1973 Fr Smyth was again sent for treatment, this time at St Patrick's Psychiatric

Hospital in Dublin. In 1974 Fr Smyth was institutionalised for a time at Stroud in Gloucestershire. In 1989
he was referred by the community for further
treatment by a Consultant Psychologist in Dublin. Fr
Smyth attended him on a regular basis until late last
year. From his history you see that we sought expert
intervention and treatment for Fr Smyth.

Fr Smyth's behaviour has perplexed and troubled
our community over many years. We always hoped
that a combination of treatment, Fr Smyth's intelligence and the grace of God would enable Fr Smyth
to overcome his disorder. We did not adequately
understand the compulsive nature of his disorder or
the serious and enduring damage which his
behaviour could cause.

Fr Smyth was born and reared in West Belfast and
had many friends there. We are aware of one
occasion only on which he was there in a pastoral
capacity. To the best of our knowledge, he was not
on any pastoral ministry when wrongdoing occurred.

On two occasions Fr Smyth was sent on temporary assignment to do parish work in America. On
neither occasion was the Bishop of the diocese to
which he was sent notified of his propensity to molest
children. On both occasions Fr Smyth offended against
young parishioners. I acknowledge that I, as his
religious superior, committed a grave error in sending
Fr Smyth abroad without warning the Bishop to whom
I sent him.

I have recently learned that between 1992 and
1993 Fr Smyth paid substantial sums of money in

response to a complaint made directly to him by the family of a young person in America. The community had no knowledge of this complaint until recently and did not make or authorise the payments or know anything about them.

The community has paid no money to any person arising out of Fr Smyth's offending.

In 1989 I received complaints from a family about Fr Smyth's conduct with their children. Twice thereafter, Cardinal Daly, then Bishop of Down and Conor, [sic] *communicated with me and requested that I, as Fr Smyth's religious superior, take appropriate steps to deal with Fr Smyth's misconduct. Dr Patrick Walsh, the present Bishop of Down and Conor* [sic]*, also contacted me regarding the same issue. After the 1989 complaint I had arranged for Fr Smyth to attend a Clinical Psychologist in Dublin regularly and so informed both Bishops. I also gave assurances to both Bishops that I would deal effectively with Fr Smyth.*

With my approval, in December 1993, Fr Marshall, one of our Community, telephoned the father of one of the young people against whom Fr Smyth had offended. Our purpose was to arrange a meeting with the young person's father to discuss Fr Smyth's offending and its possible consequences for the victim and the community.

I was not aware of any desire on the part of the RUC or the Garda Siochana to interview or serve any process upon Fr Smyth. I did not know that the extradition of Fr Smyth was sought or contemplated. Fr Smyth has not held any permanent position since his return from the United States in 1983. However, he undertook a number of assignments for short periods, the last of which was as chaplain to a hospital in Cork.

In this letter I have done my best to answer the many questions you have asked. I hope you will treat it as my response and that of our community for the purposes of your programme. The community has been devastated by these events and we can only, once again, express our heart-felt sorrow and continuing concern for all those who have been hurt.

Yours sincerely,
+Kevin A. Smith,
O. Praem. Abbot

In the end Abbot Smith was compelled to answer our questions, to make himself publicly accountable for his actions even if it was just ten days before transmission of *Suffer Little Children*. His answers fully justify the campaign for truth from the abused and their families. I heard of the Abbot's fax in a telephone box at Munich airport where I had been spending a few days with a member of the Norbertine Order at Kilnacrott Abbey, Fr Bruno Mulvihill – the priest who was master of ceremonies at Abbot Smith's inauguration in August 1969. He had become the whistle-blower on the extent of the cover-up within the Norbertine Order of Fr Smyth's paedophile past and what he had to say was devastating for the order and its hierarchy.

12

FR BRUNO: THE WHISTLE-BLOWER

I am sorry to say that the legal and media specialists who are at present trying to act on behalf of the Catholic Church in Ireland are finding it extremely difficult to get any coherent replies from the Abbot and have now concluded that there is no way in which the Abbot or any member of his council can be even permitted to appear on the [television] Programme, for their total inadequacy would be plain for everyone to see.

Cardinal Cahal Daly, 29 September 1994, in private correspondence with Fr Bruno Mulvihill, O. Praem, member of the Norbertine Order, based in County Cavan.

One Sunday morning after Mass had been celebrated in the church at Kilnacrott Abbey two figures sneaked round the back of the building for a secret puff on a cigarette and as they smoked they could hear peculiar noises coming from the sacristy. It was 1964 and according to one of the two smokers breaking abbey rules, it was already an open secret among members of the Norbertine Order based there that the priest in charge of the mass servers, Fr Smyth, had a propensity to abuse children. At the time Fr Bruno Mulvihill was a nineteen-year-old novice filled with teenage enthusiasm for what he thought was going to be a journey through life committed to the work of God. Along with his smoking partner Fr Michael McKeon he reported the noises to the then Abbot, Fr Felim Colwell, who apparently told them they were 'imagining things'. This was the first time Fr Mulvihill says he attempted to warn the abbey about Fr Smyth but not the last. Today, at the age of forty-nine, he finds himself on the verge of removal from the Norbertine Order because he became a 'whistle-blower', apparently facing the wrath of his order for daring to tell the world he spent years trying to ring alarm bells about Fr Smyth's paedophilia. 'Alas, it was all to no avail,' says Fr Mulvihill, fearful of the risk of putting more children at risk and disgusted his warnings fell on deaf ears.

Bruno Mulvihill was born on 17 July 1945 in County Galway, the elder of two sons (both destined for the priesthood) born to Elizabeth, principal of Woodlawn National School, near Ballinasloe and James, an inspector with the Department of Agriculture. The sense of vocation that led him to the abbey at Ballyjamesduff followed a visit to Garbally Park School in Ballinasloe by the late Fr Philip Nash, then novice master at Kilnacrott, who said enough to hold the attention of a young and ambitious pupil. On 8 September 1963, the young pupil in question joined the Norbertine Order at Kilnacrott as a novice.

Bruno Mulvihill took his first profession at the abbey exactly two years later, thus beginning what is regarded as a three-year trial period of self-examination during which all those hopeful of becoming priests measure themselves against the three vows taken by members of the order: poverty, chastity and obedience.

This is not done in isolation, for throughout this crucial period there was regular consultation with the abbey's master of the professed who continued to be Fr Philip Nash. Bruno Mulvihill became Fr Bruno Mulvihill at ordination in July 1971, by which time he had chosen an academic path as the appropriate means of fulfilling his religious life, having first studied philosophy and theology at St Patrick's College, Maynooth, where his favourite lay subject was ancient classics. For four years from 1970, he was in northern Germany attending the Catholic Faculty of Theology at Münster University and where he says he was privileged to study with such distinguished theologians as Karl Rahner and J. B. Metz. Clearly fascinated by the history of mankind, his next move was to Bonn in 1974 for specialised studies focused on the interaction of the ancient world and early Christianity, covering the years 400BC to 400AD. The young priest remained at Bonn until 1979, when he accepted a variety of pastoral duties, each for a short period, before finally settling down that year as a teacher of ancient church history at the Protestant Faculty of Theology at Bochum University in the Ruhr Valley. His teaching post was concluded in 1988 when he moved to the Premonstratensian Abbey at Obermedlengen, in Bavaria, for a posting which lasted just three years.

Given his obvious fascination with the ancient history of the church, it seems fitting that my first meeting with Fr Mulvihill should be on the site of one of the oldest Catholic churches in the world, one which antedates the arrival of St Patrick in Ireland. Augsburg is a small German city about an hour's drive out of Munich and it was to the parish of St Ulrich that Fr Mulvihill reported in 1991 to commence what for him was a lengthy period of pastoral work. Historians have concluded that there has been a church on this particular site in Augsburg since the year 304 AD, although it has not always been the religious focus of the local Catholic population. At one time it was a centre for Protestant worship. Four years prior to the arrival of Fr Mulvihill, the present pope visited the church which has had a Papal basilica since 1937 and which thousands visit every year to marvel at the architecture and the beautiful ornate decor.

This is the background of the man who was to reveal the extent of the cover-up taking place not only at Kilnacrott Abbey but elsewhere within the Church, the man who placed the truth of criminal wrong-doing before the interests of the Church or the order to which he belonged. By the time Fr Mulvihill arrived in Augsburg in 1991, Fr Smyth was already under police investigation and, as we shall see, Fr Mulvihill had made some startlingly accurate prophecies in his correspondence with senior Catholic clerics. It is not without irony that the conduit for our meeting was the Kilnacrott Abbey *News Letter,* distributed from the abbey to all members of its community. Its purpose was to keep them informed of the latest developments, to note the movement of priests from

Kilnacrott and to pass on anything considered news-worthy. By the end of the summer of 1994 there was one very newsworthy item to include, the conviction and jailing of a member of the order for seventeen offences of sexual abuse of children. As he scanned the latest edition in his apartment in Augsburg Fr Mulvihill's eye fell upon the brief report of Fr Smyth's recent incarceration in Her Majesty's Prison Magilligan in County Derry. Readers were informed the priest had settled in well given the circumstances and they were invited to write to Fr Smyth, his prison number listed along with the address. There was also mention of a forthcoming television documentary on the subject of Fr Smyth and to Fr Mulvihill this presented yet another opportunity to tell his story, this time publicly.

The editing of *Suffer Little Children* was already under way when the link to Fr Mulvihill was established, *Counterpoint* editor Tony Curry and I travelled to Germany on Saturday 24 September to meet this man who claimed to have an extensive knowledge of Fr Brendan Smyth's paedophile activities. We travelled in hope that this might be the breakthrough we had been seeking for several months but we brought with us a healthy scepticism. We were prepared for the worst – even for another let down in this seemingly never-ending saga.

In one of Augsburg's cobbled squares we found Fr Mulvihill's church and we settled down to two days of talking and scrutinising the priest's extensive range of correspondence. It made grim reading for anyone who still clung to the hope that leading Church officials had no prior knowledge of Fr Brendan Smyth's sexual assaults on children. We filmed on Monday 26 September before returning to Belfast late that night.

Fr Mulvihill's story about the knowledge of Fr Smyth's sexual proclivities among senior Church figures suggests that their attitude was one of indifference and disdain. 'Even as we speak,' said Fr Mulvihill, 'members of the Catholic hierarchy are running scared in the aftermath of the Fr Smyth trial, trying to put a safe distance between themselves, the activities of the paedophile priest and their knowledge of those activities.' If what Fr Mulvihill told us in Germany was true, we could see that it represented a chronicle of missed opportunities by senior Catholic churchmen of bringing about an end to further abuse of children. Prior to our unexpected journey to Germany, no one from the Church or the order was prepared to make himself available for questioning in public.

Here we had for the first time somebody who seemed prepared to be open and for whom hanging up the telephone as an escape mechanism would be unlikely. Meeting Fr Mulvihill, accepting his reasoning and his ability to use his trained mind to extract order from chaos made it easier to accept that what he was saying was true. The clinching factor was his readiness to open his files to reveal his written record of many of the warnings he gave about Fr Smyth. Hearing 'peculiar' noises from the altar boys' sacristy as far back as 1964 at a time when a known paedophile was on the prowl was hardly an auspicious start to Fr Mulvihill's life as a Norbertine and as he was to discover there was worse to follow in the years ahead.

Four years later, in 1968, Fr Mulvihill said he had been acting in an official capacity as Abbot Colwell's secretary. One morning early in 1968 he happened to be closest to the telephone when it rang in the office, so he picked it up:

It was the Bishop of Providence, Rhode Island in the United States, Russell J. McVinney. He wanted to speak to Abbot Colwell but at the time the Abbot was very seriously ill and the bishop asked me to pass on an urgent message to him after I told him I would be visiting the Abbot at his place of convalescence. He said Fr Brendan Smyth was being put on a plane back to Ireland in disgrace after it was discovered that he had been sexually abusing children in Providence, Rhode Island.

Fr Smyth had travelled to the United States some time in 1965. After seven months the local paper, the *Providence Evening Bulletin*, carried a report about the new parish priest under two short headlines, 'Favor for Bishop McVinney', and in larger type, 'Eire Priest in E. Greenwich.' The opening paragraphs of the report read:

As a gesture of generosity from Holy Trinity Abbey in County Cavan, Ireland, the Rev. Brendan Smyth has been working as a parish priest in Our Lady of Mercy Church in East Greenwich. The favor is for the Most Rev. Russell J. McVinney, D.D., Bishop of Providence, whose family came from County Cavan.

The Irish priest was described as 'speaking in a brogue

with American colloquialisms', the article informing readers that he was 'too perceptive' to generalise easily about Ireland or America. The report continues, quoting the priest:

> The Irish are building a new country since English suppression of Gaelic traditions and political domination ended in the beginning of the century.

Reporter Laurie Lisle provides a brief biographical profile of Fr Smyth, mentioning his parish work in Scotland and Wales, but not in Ireland where, as she quotes Fr Smyth, 'Priests are plentiful'. The story concludes with Fr Smyth's assessment of the 'currents of change' in the Catholic Church, with the final two paragraphs quoting the priest as saying:

> Today superiors are less authoritarian than ten years ago. For instance, I was given the choice whether to come here or not – and I was delighted at the chance. I don't look for strange places necessarily and I love to go back to places where I've worked – but a new experience wouldn't be turned down.

Sadly, as we all now know only too well, there are few places where he would be welcomed back. Three years later the *Providence Journal* covered the story of the priest's departure from Rhode Island in its edition dated 25 February 1968. Under the heading, 'Their Best Fan Is Going Home', Richard A. Beardsley wrote:

He will take with him memories both fond and perplexing and leave behind the memory of a man whose love of children and lilting 'r's and 'e's brightened the town and the lives of many in it.

Fr Smyth's interest in leisure activities are especially singled out for mention by the reporter:

Recreation, especially children's recreation, has played a big part in his stay locally. Since his arrival in the summer of 1965, he has helped rejuvenate the local CYO and given hour after hour of unofficial time to the girl scouts.

The Irish priest is quoted expressing his fondness for basketball; college and professional games on television hold his attention although he goes on to say he has 'become most enthusiastic about basketball at the parish level'. The story continues:

During his stay in East Greenwich he has organised teams for both boys and girls at Our Lady of Mercy. And last Friday night, less than a week before his departure, he was still giving his own time to be with the youngsters at the gym.

While Fr Smyth was in the United States lavishing all this attention on 'children's recreation', back home in Ireland his propensity to molest children sexually was known to his order. That was confirmed for Fr Mulvihill when he took the message from the Bishop of Providence to Abbot

Colwell who, according to Fr Mulvihill, spoke of having such problems before. Fr Smyth had 'returned to the abbey under a cloud from service in the diocese of Galloway in Scotland and the diocese of Menevia in Wales'. Whilst no one has come forward in Scotland to level allegations of abuse against the priest from Ireland who served in Annan for two years from 1957, the same cannot be said of Wales, where John Russell (his real name) says he met Fr Smyth as an eleven-year-old altar boy in 1958. Mr Russell, who now lives in Australia, went public on his allegations. He was an altar boy at St Mary's Church, Wrexham, Clwyd in North Wales. Fr Smyth was staying at the presbytery and would make an effort to befriend the altar boys, plying them with tubes of sweets in exchange for hugs. At the time Mr Russell had his sights set on becoming a priest but unfortunately for him, he made the mistake of telling Fr Smyth of his ambitions. The priest invited the boy to holiday in Ireland and visit Kilnacrott Abbey in County Cavan. The boy was delighted to accept the offer and with the opportunity to look around the abbey. Fr Smyth picked John Russell up at his home and the pair set off in the priest's car towards Holyhead to travel by ferry to Dun Laoghaire but long before the ship berthed at the Irish port, the young boy had reason to regret taking the priest up on his offer.

Once at sea Fr Smyth got the boy into a berth and here the abuses began: the priest insisted on the boy sleeping in the same bed every night, even when they got to Ireland and were staying at hotels, like the Gresham in Dublin. In fact, the only night Mr Russell got a bed to himself was during the overnight stop at Kilnacrott Abbey.

Naturally, Fr Mulvihill had no knowledge of these events in Wales in 1958 but he could confirm that Fr Smyth had just returned from a tour of duty in Wales in August 1963 when he arrived at the abbey to make his retreat prior to entry into the novitiate. It was not possible to verify Fr Mulvihill's story about Rhode Island with Abbot Colwell; he died at just fifty-four years of age on Christmas Eve, 1968, plunging a deeply saddened abbey into limbo for much of 1969 before the appointment of a successor. Before Fr Kevin Smith even had a fitting for his abbatial robes something happened which has become the subject of intense speculation as to whether a certain document exists or not. And Fr Mulvihill was to be the main actor in the drama.

After he obtained his degree in ancient classics in the autumn of 1968, there came a change in emphasis in his life. For a year he travelled daily to Navan to study theology in St Columban's College but he admits to having become profoundly bored at the kindergarten style of study. He preferred to perform such menial chores as preparing visitors' rooms, cleaning corridors or working in the sacristy. One day it was his lot to prepare a room recently vacated by Fr Brendan Smyth to accommodate a visitor.

What happened next is undoubtedly one of the most controversial events in the story of Fr Brendan Smyth because it places Fr Bruno Mulvihill in direct conflict not only with senior members of his religious order but also with some archivists at the Vatican who thus far have not been able to trace the document as described by Fr Mulvihill. It is one of the key mysteries of the whole scandal as it raises crucial questions about who knew about Fr Smyth's paedophilia and when they knew about it. What Fr Mulvihill says is that he discovered in a drawer an official document, a decree issued in Rome against Fr Smyth and issued by the Congregation for Religious, the Catholic Church body which is charged with overseeing the life of religious orders within the Church. It is this body which also deals with wayward religious. Fr Mulvihill is adamant that the decree exists and said so publicly when his view was transmitted in the programme. He told us that discovery of the document convinced him that the abbey gossip about Fr Smyth was not just speculation but was obviously founded on factual information. This is what he told us:

> I discovered the decree that had been issued by the Congregation of Religious. I think one of the terms was that his faculties for confession were to be rescinded for life and that he was not to leave the abbey precincts on his own - only in the company of a trusted priest member of the community - because he was a very real danger as far as sex abuse of children was concerned.

When I asked if these were the words he had read in the document, Fr Mulvihill said, 'Yes'. He then described where it had been found:

> I found this document in a room in which Fr Brendan had been living. He did not take this document with him. I was not expecting to find it.

> The prior was not in the house. I gave the document
> to the superior, Fr Kilian Mitchell, who put it in Fr
> Brendan's file in the Abbot's office.

According to Fr Mulvihill, this document was discovered
after the death of Abbot Colwell, but before the election
of Fr Kevin Smith as Abbot.

Two more years passed before Fr Mulvihill himself was
ordained, with Fr Brendan Smyth acting as master of
ceremonies for the occasion, and he says it was shortly
after this happened that he asked the new Abbot, Fr Smith,
about the document he claims he found:

> After my ordination in 1971, I approached Abbot
> Smith about this decree, told him I knew of its
> existence and its terms, asked him why Fr Brendan
> was driving around in a Northern Ireland registered
> car, and leaving the abbey on his own at all times.
> Abbot Smith's response was that Fr Brendan had
> been penalised enough and was a good priest. At
> that stage I gave up completely.

The day after we returned from Germany (Tuesday, 27
September 1994) I contacted Abbot Smith to thank him
for his fax of the previous day and to ask him for his
comments on the allegations being made by a member of
his community that there was a decree from Rome dating
back nearly thirty years in relation to Fr Smyth. Abbot
Smith denied all knowledge of a decree; he told me he
had never heard anyone discuss it and said that it had
never been brought to his attention, further claiming that

this was the first he had heard of any such document. I sent him a fax detailing the questions raised by allegations from Fr Bruno Mulvihill and contacted him next day. The Abbot repeated his denials of knowledge of any decree and in denying Fr Mulvihill's allegation that he had raised the issue with him after his ordination in 1971, the Abbot had this to say:

> I never, he never spoke to me about it at all. I wasn't even his boss at the time. No way, that's a complete and utter lie. I'm talking about from '69 onwards. Fr Mulvihill never talked to me. I never saw the decree, never heard of it, never got word of it until you mentioned it yesterday.

When I explained that Fr Mulvihill said he had taken a call from the United States when he was secretary to Abbot Colwell, Abbot Smith replied, 'Ah, no, bullshit.' The Abbot said Fr Mulvihill was never secretary to anyone at the abbey and advised me that as a novice he would not have had access to a decree. Bruno Mulvihill's novitiate was from 8 September 1963 until 8 September 1965.

The Abbot warned me about Fr Mulvihill, stating I should be careful about believing everything he said and pointing out that the issue of a decree was a very serious matter and even though Fr Smyth was now in prison there had been no decree from Rome. The Abbot offered some advice: 'My advice, and now it's up to yourself ... don't take that man's word, OK? 'Cause you are on very shaky ground, that's my advice to you, OK? I don't mind what you do, but if you do it you might be in trouble, OK? Right?' Next day a more formal written response arrived by fax from the abbey:

Thank you for your letter of September 27th. As I have already said, I believe that Fr Brendan Smyth commenced offending against children early in his religious life. I am unable to say with certainty if he abused children in each of the locations you mention. [Scotland, Wales and Providence Rhode Island, USA] Sadly, it is clear that Father Smyth has a very long history of offending.

I am not aware that a decree regarding Father Smyth issued from the Congregation for Institutes of Consecrated Life and Societies of Apostolic Life in Rome. Lest this may have happened prior to my appointment as Father Smyth's religious superior in 1969 I made an enquiry with this congregation. I am informed that the congregation maintains careful and complete records of such matters but that it has been unable to trace any record of a complaint or decree pertaining to Father Smyth.

Yours sincerely,
Kevin A. Smith, O. Praem, Abbot.

What is missing from Abbot Smith's accounts of events is any mention that Fr Mulvihill had been a constant thorn in the Abbey's side ever since that day he had a contraband cigarette near the altar boys' sacristy thirty years before. He did not mention two separate occasions in the early seventies when Fr Mulvihill saw the paedophile emerge from separate rooms with young children and that on both occasions these children were sobbing.

The Abbot did not indicate if he had been made aware of complaints Fr Mulvihill made to two prelates during a ceremony at Kilnacrott Abbey in 1974 to mark the golden jubilee of the property as a house of religion, one of whom was the Papal Nuncio, Archbishop Gaetano Alibrandi, who did not acknowledge receipt of Fr Mulvihill's letter. The other was the Bishop of Kilmore, Dr Francis MacKiernan, who, according to Fr Mulvihill, did not wish to discuss such a matter with a junior priest, and instead referred to his friendship with his old school friend Abbot Kevin Smith. Just after getting back from Germany I contacted Bishop MacKiernan at his home in Cavan. The time was 10.35 am on 28 September. This is the conversation:

Author: Is that Bishop MacKiernan?

Bishop: Yes.

Author: My name's Chris Moore, I'm calling from Ulster Television in Belfast. I work for *Counterpoint.* It's a current affairs programme.

Bishop: Yeah.

Author: I'm calling actually about a story we're doing on Fr Brendan Smyth from Kilnacrott Abbey.

Bishop: Yes.

Author: I'm wondering if you could help me with it; it's in relation to apparently someone we've spoken to who claims there was a decree from the Congregation for Religious and Secular Institutes in the late '60s concerning Fr Smyth. I wonder if you had any knowledge of it?

Bishop: I haven't. No. I'm afraid you'd have to contact his legal people.

Author: Right . . .

Bishop: I wouldn't know anything about it.

Author: I mean do you know of a priest called, er, Bruno Mulvihill?

Bishop: Yes, he's in Germany.

Author: He says he had a conversation with you about Fr Smyth and this decree. Do you ever recall that?

Bishop: No, I don't I do not I'm afraid. OK? Then bye, bye.

[Call terminated by Bishop at this point.]

According to Fr Mulvihill, he followed up these 1974 conversations with the two prelates by putting his concerns to them in writing but he says he never got any replies to his letters. As he continued his studies in Germany Fr Mulvihill says there was a lengthy period when he put the matter of Fr Brendan Smyth to one side, but it was revitalised during the mid-'80s when Fr Mulvihill had communications from various individuals at Kilnacrott Abbey expressing concern over the whispered stories of Fr Smyth's sexual activities with children. In 1985 a visit to the abbey by Fr Mulvihill ended with his being taken before the Abbot's Council for disciplinary action and he says this followed prolonged discussions with young members of the Norbertine Order at the abbey who were deeply concerned about, among other serious irregularities rightly giving cause for concern, the stories of Fr Smyth's sexual misconduct with children.

Fr Mulvihill was not alone during this visit; he brought

with him a German friend and for the duration of their stay they were based at the abbey, but after they returned to the continent that priest was forbidden to communicate with anyone at the abbey because of the punishment of Solemn Warning issued by the Abbot's Council. Any letters he wrote to seek removal of the disciplinary measure were ignored. There may be another reason for Abbot Smith's council admonishing the priest from Germany: during 1984 Fr Mulvihill says he made another attempt to alert those responsible within the Norbertine Order, this time travelling to an abbatial blessing in California where he met with the Abbot General of the Norbertine Order, Marcel Van de Ven and his right-hand man, Abbot Benjamin Mackin of the De Pere Abbey in Wisconsin, USA. He recounts the detail of this meeting in a letter to Abbot Smith dated 9 November 1985, in which he also complains at some length about his treatment by the Abbot and his council at Kilnacrott. Fr Mulvihill began this part of the letter by referring back to the conversations he had been having with the younger members of the Norbertine Order at the County Cavan abbey:

The main topic of conversation between those in training and me was the serious matter of Fr Brendan Smyth who apparently is not just travelling around in a Belfast-registered car but is also misusing children. This was well known as far back as 1964 when I was a novice and things have not got better. It is at present a cause of major scandal among the juniors: I brought the matter to the attention of the Abbot General and Abbot Mackin when I was in California. The reaction of the Abbot General was: 'I do not believe it,' Abbot Mackin said he would look into the matter and take it up with you. I have also discussed the matter at length with the Pater Abbas of Kilnacrott, Abbot Noyens of Tongerlo, Belgium, who said he would monitor the situation even though he could not interfere with matters pertinent to an independent canonry even if it be a daughter canonry of his own abbey. Sooner or later this bubble will burst, child misuse is a dangerous matter. I feel very hurt that you refused to talk to me about Fr Brendan when we met in Postel Abbey: you cut me off and asserted that Fr Brendan was a zealous priest who had done a lot of good work in many dioceses around the world and who had 'had a problem in the past.' You seem to think that this sexual orient-ation is a matter which one can lay off as easily as a shirt, this is a misguided approach. Over and above that, Father Brendan is a brash man who has wound you around his little finger: some fine day these children will have psychic problems which we cannot now foresee and may not want to be bribed into silence. It is not for any personal reason that I am documenting this now: should the bubble burst at any stage, then I have my documentation. My protest is timely, to have answered it by forbidding me to speak to particularly those members of the community who are genuinely concerned because they do not know if it is wise to bind themselves to a community where such a man can have free play is nothing short of being utterly irresponsible.

Fr Mulvihill concluded the letter by warning that should knowledge of the Fr Smyth affair ever become public, he would use his letters and other documentation at his own discretion to provide proof that he had taken the right steps at the right time. Prophetic words indeed from someone who says he is motivated solely by his disgust of paedophilia and his desire to protect children from abuse by a trusted member of his own order. It was a warning call which seems to have been ignored by a number of the superiors who were the addressees of this letter. Perhaps if they had taken action, children like Alison, her brother and her cousin would not have been forced to endure the unwelcome attentions of the paedophile priest while they were using the children's library at Kilnacrott. Admittedly, their experiences happened in the late fifties, before Fr Mulvihill began his personal crusade against the paedophile but, as we know now, the Norbertine Order knew of the priest's 'propensity early in his religious life'. Alison acknowledges she was one of the lucky ones, but even though the interference from Fr Smyth was mild in her case, she hated having to see him inside the abbey every time she went there for her library book. This is her story:

> I come from a very religious family and so we all visited the abbey at Kilnacrott. I was there quite a bit as a child, attending devotions or going to concerts, and I liked going to the children's library they had. It was here that I met Fr Smyth. When we returned our books he would take time to ask us how we got on with the book, just chatting about

the story. He was always pulling my ear or
squeezing my nose. It hurt a bit sometimes but then
he would ask me to go into a small room off the
library where there was a table and chairs. In here
he would lift me up on to his knee and then he
would turn me over, lift my skirt and slap my
bottom. This went on for a year when I was eleven
years of age, that would have been around 1957.
He always lifted my skirt and I did not like it but I
told no one about it. Every time he did this he would
give me loads of sweets he kept in another room.
Once he had finished with me he would open the
door to let me out to pick my next book and then
he would take my brother into the room. What we
did not realise until the whole Fr Smyth story broke
last year on television was that he had been
interfering with my brother as well. In fact, there
was a gathering of the family last year at about the
time the Smyth story hit the headlines and during
conversation at that meeting, I discovered that my
brother and two other men (one is my cousin and
another very close family friend) all had problems
with the priest. You can imagine the shock of sitting
chatting and suddenly discovering that four people
in the room had difficulties with Fr Smyth. My
cousin said the priest fondled him, his private parts.
He said he could not go to his family because he
did not think they would believe him. They were all
afraid to speak up against Fr Smyth. I have not gone
to the police because what happened to me was so
minor by comparison to what others had to endure

and there are good priests at the abbey, very good priests and I would not want to hurt them. He was a very bad apple and I hate him. Some time around 1957 or 1958 he disappeared off the scene and it was seven years before I saw him again. He asked my mother about me when he got back and he asked to see me, to offer me extra lessons to help with my Latin. But this time before I went to the abbey I made sure there was someone with me ... I took my sister and would not let her out of my sight. She doesn't know why, but that was my way of making sure I was not alone with him. I was eighteen years of age at this point, but I just did not want to be alone with the priest in his room. From that day he has never spoken to me and even though he still called at our house regularly to see my father, he would ignore me completely. I hate the man.

Given Fr Smyth's track record as a paedophile, it seems unlikely that Alison and her relatives were the last local children to face abuse inside the abbey, but precisely when the priest finally stopped his abuses there is impossible to determine. In order to get reaction to Fr Mulvihill's story that he had spoken to the superior general of the Norbertine Order in 1984, I tried to make contact with Abbot General Marcel Van de Ven. But tracking him down has not been an easy task and it proved to be impossible prior to transmission of our programme. I resumed my search for him early in 1995, tracing him via his home abbey of Berne in Holland to an abbey in the United States but just missing him by minutes; then to a private house in Canada where he declined to engage in any conversation about Fr Brendan Smyth in the presence of his hosts and finally, on 6 February 1995 to a restaurant of some kind within the Vatican itself. He told me he did not believe a decree had ever been issued against Fr Smyth and said his office could find no trace of it when conducting a search in the Vatican. He also told me he would not be prepared to record a television interview, stating that enough had already been said in statements issued to the media in the aftermath of the Fr Smyth story breaking in the autumn of 1994.

Author: What I am interested in is to find out if there is a possibility that we could come and do an interview with you in Rome about this matter.

Abbot General: No, no, no, I don't do that.

Author: Why not?

Abbot General: There has been enough publicity . . . I, eh, I eh, don't do it and I, I, will be away from Rome for three weeks . . .

Author: Doesn't the order feel that someone should be answerable, I mean no one has really gone on record on television to speak on behalf of the order to explain what went wrong with Fr Brendan's case.

Abbot General: That, that is the duty of the Abbey of Kilnacrott eh, as I told you, I, I, I, know only since April or May and I now, I, I, feel sorry for the families and so on and I said that but I'm not going to speak on television, I have said . . .

Author: Why don't you say sorry in front of a television audience, why won't you say sorry there?

Abbot General: I, I have said that to so many newspapers that the people know that . . .

Abbot General Van de Ven said he knew nothing of the money which Fr Smyth sent to the family in the United States and expressed doubt that this was true but said he would be concerned if it were so because members of the Norbertine Order took a vow of poverty.

Abbot General: If . . . if this is true that he paid, was it twenty thousand dollars? . . . I don't know . . . I can only say that is not correct. We have a vow of poverty and of communal life.

Author: But he did pay twenty thousand dollars – that is correct.

Abbot General: Are you sure?

Author: Yes. I have spoken to the people who have received the money.

Abbot General: I see, I see . . .

Author: And I've spoken to their lawyer and the money was paid in four equal payments of five thousand dollars each time and at an interval of six months.

Abbot General: Yes, yes . . .

Author: How could he accumulate such money?

Abbot General: Yeah, yeah, I can only say that it's against his vow of poverty like, like what he did with the children is against his vow of chastity, but yeah, people do it. But I agree that according to our vows it would be impossible if he had twenty thousand dollars for sure.

Author: And have you tried to find out where he got the money?

Abbot General: No. No.

Author: What do you intend to do about Fr Smyth if you say he was working against his vow of poverty by having such wealth? And if you say he went against his vow of chastity by abusing children, why isn't he being removed from the order?

Abbot General: I will wait the outcome finally when the cases are, em ... eh ... there are accusations against him. I don't know what will come out in the court cases and then I will, I will surely handle what I think I have to do. I am about to say that I cannot remove him from the order: that has to go to the Vatican. Of course, I can say something to the Vatican but I cannot remove him ... because some newspapers have asked me that also. That I cannot ... I have not ... that's beyond my jurisdiction so to say.

Amazingly, this was not the only area of authority over which the Abbot General told me during this conversation that he did not have jurisdiction. He also claimed that he did not have the authority over an abbey because to use his words, 'Our abbeys are autonomous and I, in the first place, I am the delegate or the representative of the order in Rome, but I have not immediate jurisdiction on the abbey.'

This was the second time I was informed of the authority of the Abbot as major superior of an abbey. The other was in a letter from Cardinal Daly, dated 26 August

1994, when he finally washed his hands of Kilnacrott Abbey. Cardinal Daly had, I thought, taken his time in preparing his letter to me, I had first written on May 20 and by 15 August I felt it was time to prompt him again with a letter asking him to reconsider his and the Church's decision not to make anyone available for interview. In the meantime, however, I learned from other sources that he was genuinely out of circulation for a considerable time due to a prolonged and painful illness.

In spite of my request for the Church to provide someone to answer publicly to its people, there is no change in the position adopted by the Abbot or the Cardinal. In his letter of 26 August, Cardinal Daly acknowledged the 'immense hurt caused to many people over a long number of years' by Fr Smyth and he said he was acutely aware of the impact of sexual abuse on the natural development of a child or adolescent. He wrote of the 'exploitation by a priest of the trust placed in him by a child' as an 'appalling occurrence', adding:

Fr Smyth's conviction and imprisonment is, I believe, a painful but important step in the vindication of those children against whom he offended. I fervently hope and pray that each who has suffered will, in time and with help, recover from what has happened.

But when it came to dealing with the specifics of our programme, what the Cardinal said was that what happened at the abbey was beyond his control:

In the context of your programme and the specific issues which it addresses, I believe it is important that you understand the particular position which a member of a Religious Order holds within the structure of the Catholic Church. Whilst Diocesan Priests are directly subject to the authority of the Bishop of the Diocese in which they are incardinated, the position for members of religious orders is different. They are subject as regards disciplinary matters to the Superior of their Order. Accordingly at all relevant times Fr Smyth was, as he still remains, bound under obedience and subject to authority and rule of his Superior, Abbot Kevin Smith of Holy Trinity Abbey. In the light of that fact I do not feel it is appropriate for me to comment on the facts of this particular case.

The Cardinal's candour was the clearest indication yet that he did not want to accept any blame. The Abbot was being hung out to dry. There was no further doubt in my mind that this was being put forward as official policy. No one from the abbey or the Church ever did make themselves available for our programme but after it had been transmitted the Cardinal and other Irish bishops were suddenly confronted by an outraged public and they were forced into making themselves publicly accountable. The public's outrage turned to anger when Fr Smyth's postings to hospitals in Cork and Kerry were made known and Cardinal Daly found himself being questioned about the whole affair on RTE radio on 16 October 1994. He was asked if he could understand how people could say, as the Minister for Health Brendan Howlin had said, that he was shocked to learn this was allowed to happen. Speaking on the telephone from Rome, the Cardinal said he too was as shocked as anyone could possibly be, adding he was appalled to think that over such a long period of time this priest was tragically allowed to go from place to place wreaking havoc. He described this issue as one of the most distressing he had had to deal with in his experience as a bishop.

The message was clear: the Catholic Church in Ireland, its bishops and even the Cardinal had no mandate of control over a priest in a religious order and could only make representations to the superior of the order to seek remedy of the problem. That being the case, however, how then could the Catholic Church in Ireland forbid the Abbot at Kilnacrott – or any member of his council – to appear before television cameras to answer questions about their handling of the Fr Smyth affair. At least that is one possible interpretation of the facts as explained by Cardinal Daly in his reply to a letter from Fr Mulvihill, dated 24 August 1994.

Fr Mulvihill told the Cardinal that the scandal surrounding the paedophile priest was not an isolated matter but that the burden of guilt must be shared by those superiors who permitted ongoing crime. Fr Mulvihill took the opportunity to repeat his efforts to gain the attention of Abbot General Norbert Calmels and Abbot General Marcel Van de Ven. He mentioned also his efforts to attract the attention of Bishop MacKiernan of Kilmore and Papal Nuncio Archbishop Gaetano Alibrandi which produced no results.

Pressure of work and illness delayed Cardinal Daly's

response to Fr Mulvihill but eventually on 29 September 1994 he replied to say that because of the fact Fr Smyth pleaded guilty no evidence was called at his trial. This meant there was as yet little public attention focused on the case. The Cardinal went on to say that this would change soon with transmission of a UTV programme which would show from research that every place Fr Smyth served coincided exactly with his areas of abuse. This was in fact a massive incrimination of the conduct of Fr Brendan Smyth's religious superiors and their collaborators. Cardinal Daly told Fr Mulvihill that in his view the programme would have the potential of being a dreadful exposure of inner-ecclesiastical modes of operation which in this case would focus on a malfunctioning abbey, its present head and his consistent failure over a long period of years to take necessary and effective action against Fr Smyth.

According to Fr Mulvihill the Cardinal was deeply concerned about the lack of reasoned explanation from the Abbot and his council and to quote Fr Mulvihill:

He expressed his sorrow that the legal and media specialists of the Catholic Church in Ireland were finding it extremely difficult to get any coherent replies from the Abbot and had therefore concluded that there was no way in which the Abbot or any member of his council could even be permitted to appear on the television programme for their total inadequacy would be plain for everyone to see.

13

A GOVERNMENT FALLS

*I have taken this decision for the good of the country,
in the interests of stability and in particular to ensure
the continuation of the peace process . . . In the
circumstances that have led to this decision I simply
wish to state that it was never, never my intention
to mislead the Dáil or withhold any material information from it. I sought a deeper investigation of the
circumstances surrounding the handling of the
Father Brendan Smyth extradition case from the new
Attorney-General and have been prepared to draw
the appropriate conclusions without flinching.*

*Taoiseach Albert Reynolds announcing his resig-
nation, 17 November 1994.*

My wife Fiona and I had Saturday, 12 November 1994,
clearly mapped out: first we would enjoy a lie-in, with
breakfast in bed, of course; then Fiona would go shopping
while I sacrificed my weekly golf outing in order to work
on the manuscript for this book. We had just managed to

enjoy boiled eggs and toast when the balloon went up, with news from Dublin that the coalition government was looking decidedly shaky because of a row over the extradition warrants for Fr Smyth. The telephone overheated as friends and colleagues, and some of the families of those Fr Smyth abused, made contact with details or questions about the developments in Dublin.

If there was to be a storm and possibly a new government in the Republic I wanted to be in Dublin to witness whatever was going to unfold. By three o'clock on the afternoon of 12 November we were both packing our bags for the hundred-mile journey south to Dublin and for what turned out to be a truly remarkable week in Irish politics. To be truthful it was difficult for me to absorb the dramatic events, for in ten years in newspapers and fifteen years in broadcasting on both radio and television, I had never experienced anything like this before. In my experience once stories were written and printed or transmitted, that was the end of them. It was time to move on to the next story. Six weeks after transmission of our report there was a very real threat that a government was about to fall because of one of the issues we had raised in the report concerning extradition warrants for Fr Smyth.

On the way to Dublin, Ken Reid, UTV's political correspondent, gave us the inside track on the dilemma facing the coalition partnership of Albert Reynolds of Fianna Fáil and his Tánaiste, Dick Spring of the Labour Party. Following our revelation on 6 October that the extradition warrants issued by the RUC in the last week of April 1993 had been sent to the Republic but never acted upon, questions were raised in the Dáil and the answers given in the house did not satisfy members sitting on the opposition benches. Perhaps most important of all, they did not satisfy those sharing power with the Taoiseach, with the Tánaiste demanding a full and proper explanation from the Attorney-General Harry Whelehan as to why there had been undue delay in executing the warrants.

The day before, a written explanation had been furnished to the cabinet from Mr Whelehan which did not go far enough for the six Labour ministers in the government. They decided to walk out of that cabinet meeting when Mr Reynolds revealed that he intended to go ahead with plans to appoint Mr Whelehan to the most senior High Court position, its Presidency. Mr Spring and his colleagues were determined to have Mr Whelehan appear before the cabinet to answer their questions about his handling of the whole affair. But as soon as they left the room, the remainder of the cabinet – all ministers from the Fianna Fáil party – agreed to the appointment of Mr Whelehan and this was a red flag to their Labour Party partners in government, who saw it as an act taken in undue haste.

Dick Spring and his Labour cabinet colleagues were furious when they learned of what they regarded as the stroke pulled by their government partners. Spring announced an emergency meeting of Labour's parliament- ary party for Sunday 13 November. Our political corres- pondent had lived in Cork for some years and knew Mr Spring rather well, and so as we sped towards Dublin he set out Mr Spring's alternatives as he had been given them by the man himself a few hours earlier. Labour's alternatives appeared to be: accept a full statement of explanation from the Taoiseach in the Dáil and kiss and make up with their government partners; decide that Labour could no longer trust their partners in government and so try to establish a rainbow coalition with Fine Gael and the other parties in opposition, such as Democratic Left and Progressive Democrats; withdraw from government, thereby precipitating a very unwelcome general election.

As Ken saw it, options one and two were the most likely pathways to peace; nobody would gain in an election and almost certainly Labour would lose a substantial number of seats. Labour's parliamentary party debated the issue behind closed doors for nearly seven hours that Sunday and at the end leader Dick Spring emerged to tell RTE television in a room packed with journalists that he had been given the full backing of his parliamentary colleagues to take whatever action he deemed appropriate. Mr Spring took this opportunity to say the failure to extradite Fr Smyth could only be seen as a serious breach of public responsibility, compounded by a serious breach of public accountability, for which no one had yet offered an explanation.

Next day the newspapers were gloomily predicting a general election. My colleagues and I attempted to keep pace with a drama which seemed capable of changing direction hourly.

Although I had covered stories in Dublin in the past I had never before been inside the Dáil and needed to secure a special one-day pass permitting me temporarily to join reporters in a packed press gallery. I was fortunate on Monday 14 November to meet an old acquaintance at the news conference which followed that day's meeting between Mr Spring and the Northern Ireland Secretary of State, Sir Patrick Mayhew. Joe Carroll a Dáil lobbyist and writer for *The Irish Times* promised to make sure I would be admitted. At twilight on Monday it was clear the Taoiseach would address parliament next day in an attempt to placate the house and save his government partnership with Mr Spring's party.

A nation waited once again, the air thick with rumours and counter-rumours as everyone paused to hear what the Taoiseach could say that might salvage the coalition whilst at the same time restoring some of the credibility destroyed during the preceding four days. Mr Reynolds began speaking around three o'clock that afternoon.

By the time he had finished, it seemed as though he might just have done enough to survive and to save the country from a pre-Christmas election but next morning as TDs gathered at the Dáil the condition of the patient took a turn for the worse as whispers reverberated around parliament that a document had been found. A document? What kind of document? What did it say? What significance does it have? Who will be embarrassed most?

By lunchtime on Wednesday, 16 November, Paul Robinson and myself were driving north towards Belfast to begin editing our tapes for the programme next evening, listening intently to news updates on RTE radio about the mysterious document. Eventually, the mystery document was identified as that detailing the case of another paedophile, John Anthony Duggan, from County Galway, who was extradited from Ireland to England in May 1992. According to Mr Spring, the Taoiseach had failed to provide the Dáil with information in his Tuesday address even though he had the information in his possession on the previous day. This was the issue which led to Mr Reynolds resignation on Thursday 17 November shortly after Mr Spring and his Labour ministers had resigned from government. Before this remarkable day ended, Mr Harry Whelehan had resigned his post as president of the High Court, just six days after he received his seal of office. Even though this had been the issue which sparked the government crisis, Mr Whelehan's resignation came too late to save Mr Reynolds and the coalition government.

There is little doubt now that the Catholic Church in Ireland was found wanting. By failing to confront the Fr Brendan Smyth affair head-on it had made itself look guilty. To suggest that the story had been blown out of all proportion was yet another attempt to mislead the public. It cut no ice, however, in those areas of society in the Republic where the evidence of involvement of Church members is clearly visible. For example, in the Rape Crisis Centre in Dublin, staff had become accustomed over the years to dealing with the fallout of an abusing priest. They had witnessed the Church policy of moving these offenders to another diocese rather than report them to the police. There was a significant increase in calls from men saying they had been abused by priests in the aftermath of the *Counterpoint* programme. In the period from 18 November to 6 December 1994, 37 per cent of the men contacting the Rape Crisis Centre were claiming abuse by a clerics; the figure for women was 18 per cent.

There seems to be an attitude problem in the Church: it must get rid of the idea that moving the priest away from the area where the offence has taken place is appropriate action. The Church must be seen to operate within the law. Changes must come, if only to remove the widespread perception among its own flock that it has for many years got away with the policy of moving people around to protect its own good name. What senior clerics must realise is that their own people now view this policy with contempt and perhaps because of Fr Smyth more people will be prepared to speak out and seek help. That help must be made available and the Church must be made to realise that its people want openness and public accountability, not excuses and policies of containment and secrecy.

If anyone were looking towards the Norbertine Order at Kilnacrott Abbey in County Cavan for a constructive lead they would be sadly disappointed. After transmission of *Suffer Little Children* the position of Abbot Kevin Smith became more and more untenable and eventually he offered his resignation. An announcement was made on Sunday 23 October, although his resignation did not become effective until noon on 27 October. But there was an important visitor to the abbey on Monday 24 October. This was the vicar of the Abbot General, Abbot Benjamin T. Mackin. During the afternoon he addressed a gathering of the entire community. Judging by the copy of the address he intended to deliver (I have no way of knowing if he delivered it word for word as it was written) there is little change in the attitude of the Norbertine Order to the events surrounding Fr Brendan Smyth. There is no mention in the entire address of those abused by the paedophile member of their order and members of the order are also warned not to speak to the media about recent events.

The Abbot explains that although 'we live out our lives in autonomous canonries,' everyone is bound in charity, in spirituality and in human relationships with all who share a common profession, follow the Rule of St Augustine and follow St Norbert in the steps of Christ Jesus. The Abbot then heaps praise on the man who had been publicly held accountable by the Catholic Church in Ireland and its hierarchy for failure to act effectively to deal with the paedophile priest:

> I have followed the situation since April. I am aware of the advice given early on by your solicitors that Abbot Smith consider his position in view of matters indicated in the council minutes. He did follow that advice and gave due consideration to that advice. He chose to carry on and he did so manfully. However, there came a time which he could not have anticipated, when that was no longer possible. At that time he made the decision to retire from office. That tells you the honesty and humility of your Abbot. I trust that you will fully appreciate his decision. It is an honest and straightforward decision made more for you than for himself.

Praise indeed for the man who successfully covered up the activities of Fr Brendan Smyth for many years, moving him from one place to another risking the possibility that the priest continue to shatter and break young lives. Seemingly Abbot Smith hung on to office even after getting some legal advice. Are these the actions of a man fit to lead a community, setting what he no doubt regarded was a fine example to the young men of the Norbertine Order at Kilnacrott who entered the priesthood to be honest, upstanding citizens serving the good of the people through God's works? But lest the community misunderstood Abbot Smith's motivation, Abbot Mackin went further, to explain something 'not often told to a community', as he put it. He informed his audience that not every member of the community has a right to know everything that goes into the decisions of abbots and councils, that there are other considerations such as the good name of individuals and of the entire community.

This seemed a fitting time to remind those present that only 'prepared statements' would be made to the media, and only from those designated to make them, the Abbot General and Fr Gerard Cusack, the new administrator of the abbey, who would hold the powers of a prelate of the order until such times as the hierarchy determined it was appropriate to permit the election of the third Abbot of Kilnacrott. If there was to be any hope of the Norbertine Order in County Cavan setting new standards of openness and public accountability in the aftermath of the shameful Fr Smyth affair, what Abbot Mackin said next killed off that hope. He was describing the events leading up to the acceptance of Abbot Smith's resignation on 21 October after hurried consultations with the definitors of the order (the small group of abbots who act as the Abbot General's counsellors):

> The people charged with making the statements were
> also instructed as to how to deal with the press and
> media. You saw this past weekend how the press and

media continued to twist the story and to do so, in my opinion, for only two reasons – as an attack on the Church (frankly they could care less for Kilnacrott itself) and for the purpose of selling newspaper and television ads. That is my opinion. But understanding the press is a lesson in itself . . . don't believe all you hear or read. What deliberately was not released to the public was the time at which the resignation-retirement would become effective.

It would seem from Abbot Mackin's address – and as I have stated, I was not present to hear it, although I am assured he gave this speech – that the order has learned nothing from its experiences. It would seem the press and media have twisted the entire story out of proportion but then Abbot Mackin appeared not to have any regard for the facts of the case. He completely ignores in this speech the wrongdoing of the priest and never suggests that it was wrong of the Abbot to cover up for his activities and by doing so put other children at risk of having their lives forever scarred. It was as if we in the press and media had made the whole thing up to attack the Church and get money from advertising! At no stage does Abbot Mackin acknowledge inappropriate behaviour from those charged with responsibility for the paedophile priest. Indeed, at no point does he even mention those who were abused by Fr Smyth.

They were the people who sought help from the press and media to give voice to the evil activities which had marked them for life. It is hardly surprising that people like Sally, Susan, Siobhan, Sarah, John, Anthony and others felt hurt by Church leaders who ignored them even after they had gone to the police with their stories. The hierarchy appeared not to want to know them. After our programme was transmitted Sally began a crusade to pressurise Cardinal Daly at least to acknowledge her pain and suffering. She wrote demanding answers to questions about the Cardinal's knowledge of the paedophile priest and when it appeared her letter was also being ignored she began telephoning the Cardinal's office to warn them if she did not hear from the Cardinal she would go public.

Sally was making the tea in her kitchen at around half past five on Boxing Day 1994 when the telephone rang. She was stunned to hear Cardinal Daly's voice. He was calling in response to her letters and telephone calls, apologising for the delay in writing back to her. His Eminence spent a few minutes expressing his profound regret that Sally had been left to suffer the consequences of the wrongdoing of a Catholic priest, a priest he had first learned of back in 1989. Yet this was the first time the spiritual leader of the Catholic people in Ireland had spoken directly to one of those abused in the Fr Smyth case.

Chris Moore
Belfast
March 1995